THE LANGUAGE GYM
SPEAKING BOOKLET II

FRENCH
SENTENCE BUILDERS
TRILOGY
PART 2

A lexicogrammar approach

SPEAKING BOOKLET

About the authors

Gianfranco Conti taught for 25 years at schools in Italy, the UK and in Kuala Lumpur, Malaysia. He has also been a university lecturer, holds a Master's degree in Applied Linguistics and a PhD in metacognitive strategies as applied to second language writing. He is now an author, a popular independent educational consultant and professional development provider. He has written around 2,000 resources for the TES website, which have awarded him the Best Resources Contributor in 2015. He has co-authored the best-selling and influential book for world languages teachers, "The Language Teacher Toolkit" and "Breaking the sound barrier: Teaching learners how to listen", in which he puts forth his Listening As Modelling methodology. Gianfranco writes an influential blog on second language acquisition called The Language Gym, co-founded the interactive website language-gym.com and the Facebook professional group Global Innovative Language Teachers (GILT). Last but not least, Gianfranco has created the instructional approach known as E.P.I. (Extensive Processing Instruction).

Dylan Viñales has taught for 15 years, in schools in Bath, Beijing and Kuala Lumpur in state, independent and international settings. He lives in Kuala Lumpur. He is fluent in five languages, and gets by in several more. Dylan is, besides a teacher, a professional development provider, specialising in E.P.I., metacognition, teaching languages through music (especially ukulele) and cognitive science. In the last five years, together with Dr Conti, he has driven the implementation of E.P.I. in one of the top international schools in the world: Garden International School. This has allowed him to test, on a daily basis, the sequences and activities included in this book with excellent results (his students have won language competitions both locally and internationally). He has designed an original Spanish curriculum, bespoke instructional materials, based on Reading and Listening as Modelling (RAM and LAM). Dylan co-founded the fastest growing professional development group for modern languages teachers on Facebook, Global Innovative Languages Teachers, which includes over 12,000 teachers from all corners of the globe. He authors an influential blog on modern language pedagogy in which he supports the teaching of languages through E.P.I. Dylan is the lead author of Spanish content on the Language Gym website and oversees the technological development of the site.

Ronan Jézéquel has taught for 15 years, in schools in Frimley, Brighton and Kuala Lumpur in state and international settings. He lives in Sabah, Malaysia. He is fluent in three languages and gets by in several more. Ronan is, besides a teacher, a keen mountain biker and an outdoor enthusiast. In the last five years, together with Dr Conti and Dylan Viñales, he has contributed to the implementation of E.P.I. in one of the top international schools in the world: Garden International School. This has allowed him to test, on a daily basis, the sequences and activities included in this book with excellent results. Ronan is the lead author of French content on The Language Gym website, and he also brings the competitive element from his sporty background to TLG with the design of live games and features such as our leaderboard.

Acknowledgements

We would like to thank our editors Aurélie Lethuilier and Jérôme Nogues for their tireless work, proofreading, editing and advising on French Sentence Builders – TRILOGY – Part 2, upon which this book is based. They are talented, accomplished professionals who work at the highest possible level and add value at every stage of the process. Not only this, but they are also lovely, good-humoured colleagues who go above and beyond, and make the hours of collaborating a real pleasure.

Thanks to Flaticon.com for providing access to a limitless library of engaging icons, clipart and images, which we have used to make this book more user-friendly and engaging for students.

As always, a huge shoutout to our team of incredible educators who helped in checking, and re-checking all the units of this volume: Darren Lester, Barry Agnew, Joanna Asse-Drouet, Becky Roberts, Victoria Harrison, Dawn Michael & Sev Bouclier. It is thanks to your time, patience, professionalism and detailed feedback that we have been able to produce such a refined and highly accurate product. Your team spirit and good-humour throughout the process also make it a real pleasure to work together.

Finally, our gratitude to the MFL Twitterati for their ongoing support of E.P.I. and the Sentence Builders book series.

Merci à tous,
Gianfranco, Dylan & Ronan

Dedication

For Catrina
-Gianfranco

For Ariella & Leonard
-Dylan

For Mariana
-Ronan

Introduction

Hello and welcome to our second Speaking Skills book, designed to be an accompaniment to our French, Extensive Processing Instruction course.

How to use this book

This book has been designed as a resource to use in conjunction with the E.P.I. approach and teaching strategies in a bid to scaffold oral communication by gradually moving from highly structured tasks (e.g. 'Oral Ping-Pong', 'No Snakes No Ladders', 'Communicative drills') to semi-structured ones (e.g. 'Surveys', 'Things in Common', 'Detectives and Informants').

The activities in this book should be carried out after an intensive listening and reading phase, in which the students have been flooded with highly comprehensible input containing the target vocabulary and grammar structures, thereby processing them receptively many times over.

If following the MARS EARS framework, teachers may want to stage two or three 'chunking-aloud' games, such as 'Mind reading', 'Sentence stealer', 'Lie detector', etc. in order to warm the students up, consolidate good pronunciation and refine their decoding skills.

Also, prior to playing oral retrieval practice games such as 'Oral Ping-Pong', it is recommended that the students do some retrieval practice in writing. This can be done through digital tools, worksheets, mini whiteboards and may be teacher and/or student led.

Finally, it is recommended that, before carrying out the fluency-building games 'Faster', 'Fast and Furious', 'Fluency cards' and Trapdoor', the students be given a few minutes to plan the tasks individually or with peers in order to decrease the potential for cognitive overload and subsequent errors that speaking at increasing speed rate may elicit due to the challenging nature of the task.

What's inside

The book contains 13 units which concern themselves with specific communicative functions, such as 'Saying what I do at home', 'Talking about my weekend plans' or 'Making after-school plans with a friend'.

Each unit includes a sentence builder with the target constructions and vocabulary followed by a series of tried and tested Conti E.P.I. speaking games, sequenced so as to pose a gradually increasing degree of challenge. The speaking games included are:

- o Oral Ping-Pong
- o Find Someone Who
- o No Snakes No Ladders
- o Staircase Translation
- o Faster!
- o Fast & Furious

- o Communicative Drills
- o Fluency Cards
- o Trapdoor
- o Things in Common
- o Detectives & Informants
- o Information Gap Tasks

As already noted, the above games are sequenced in ascending order of linguistic and cognitive challenge. The focus is on gradually building up students' fluency and autonomous competence. These games fall in the 'Structured Production', 'Routinization' and 'Spontaneity' phases in Dr Conti's **MARS EARS** pedagogical cycle, which is central to his E.P.I. approach.

Many thanks for reading this. We hope that both you and your students will find this book useful and enjoyable.

Gianfranco, Dylan & Ronan

SENTENCE BUILDERS TRILOGY - PART 2
SPEAKING BOOKLET
TABLE OF CONTENTS

How to play the games – INSTRUCTIONS

ORAL PING-PONG
Students work with a partner.
1. Student A starts by reading out his/her first sentence **in English**. Student B must translate **into French**.
2. Student A checks the answer on their sheet. If correct, Student B gets 3 points (100% accurate), 2 points (1 error), or 1 point (correct verb).
3. Student B then reads out his/her first sentence **in English**, Student A translates, and B checks and so on. It is called 'Oral ping-pong translation' because students are firing phrases at each other to translate and score points. **The person with the most points after 10 minutes wins.**
NOTE: As a follow-up, students should **write** the translations in the gaps provided.

FIND SOMEONE WHO
1. Students are each given a card and a grid to fill in (both provided in each unit of this book).
2. Students must take turns asking the key questions (also provided) and then listening to the information provided by fellow students on their cards.
3. If a student finds someone who matches the criteria in the grid, they write down the person's name.
TIP: you will need to set high expectations and then monitor students to make sure they engage in target language and use their speaking & listening skills. Some students may try and bend the rules by copying from friends.

NO SNAKES NO LADDERS
Students work in triads. You will need one dice per table and a copy of both the English & French board.
1. One student is the referee and two students are the players.
2. The referee has access to the translations (via a copy of either the English or the French board).
3. Students role a dice and then move their counter forward. They must then translate the language in the box where their counter falls.
4. If a student translates correctly (as confirmed by the referee), they can roll again.
5. If a student cannot translate the content of a square, the referee must tell them the answer, and it is then the other player's turn.
6. When a student wins the game, the referee changes, in order to allow students to alternate roles.
TIP: We recommend starting from **Target Language to English**, and then, after a couple of rounds (or whenever students are ready), working from English to Target Language.

STAIRCASE TRANSLATION
Students work with a partner.
1. Students must **translate aloud** the paragraph as quickly as possible.
2. Once the whole paragraph has been successfully translated aloud, students write down the translation into the box.

FASTER
Students alternate the role of player and referee.
1. Students translate aloud a number of sentences in front of a referee.
2. The student referee provides a time score and some feedback on accuracy.
3. The student listens to feedback and then repeats the process with a second, third, fourth referee with an aim of improving in terms of speed and accuracy on each attempt.
 TIP: Make sure that referees have a visible timer to increase motivation!

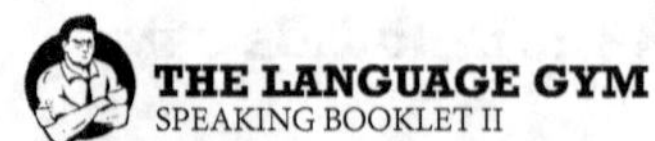

FAST & FURIOUS

Similar to FASTER, but students work from gapped target language sentences.

COMMUNICATIVE DRILLS

Students alternate the role of player and referee.
1. Students work with a partner to translate short dialogues from English to French.
2. The student referee monitors the game and provides help and feedback on accuracy.
3. Once the students have correctly translated all the boxes out loud, the game is over.

TIPS:
- We recommend a rule that whenever the game ends, the referee then faces the winner, or the loser.
- This game can be played with both players working together to translate the squares (collaborating and helping each other), or as a timed challenge (if students are more confident) to translate all 6/9 squares individually with the fastest time.

FLUENCY CARDS

Students alternate the role of player and referee.
Played like FASTER, students create sentences in the Target Language to match the content of the stimulus grid. There is a mixture of text and images in order to create varied & multi-modal connections to the lexical items and structures being studied.

THINGS IN COMMON

This activity works like the final SURVEY activity, but focuses on asking closed questions, such as "do you prefer *football* or *basketball?*"
1. Students are given some time to think about their own answers to the questions.
2. Students then ask their peers the questions and make a note of any students that have matching answers (hence 'things in common').

TIPS: Students can be given a set time to speak to as many of their peers as possible, or a race to find a certain number of people with a certain number of things in common.

TRAPDOOR

Students alternate the role of player and referee. Played like FASTER, students translate a set of sentences using the information in the table, which is chunked into several columns as a support.

DETECTIVES & INFORMANTS

This is a collaborative class game along the lines of **Find Someone Who**.
1. Divide the class into halves.
2. One half - **the detectives**: they have a grid with missing information that they need to fill in. There is one grid per team. This grid must stay at a central location, such as a team home base.
3. One half – **the informants**: they have the answers to the questions.
4. The detectives must ask questions to the informants and then return to their home base to help their team fill in the grid.

INFORMATION GAP TASK

Without viewing the other person's table, two students need to complete their own table by asking each other questions in French in order to fill in the gaps.
1. Students take turns to ask each other questions and fill in the answers.
2. The game ends when both tables are fully filled in.

SURVEY

Students ask each other the key questions that have been practised throughout the unit. They then note down key information, either in English or in French on their grid. As a follow-up you could ask students to write a summary of a friend's information, either in first or third person.

Unit 1.
Talking about the weather & free time

Que fais-tu pendant ton temps libre?		*What do you do in your free time?*
Que fais-tu quand il fait beau/mauvais?		*What do you do when the weather is good/bad?*
Que fait ton ami(e) pendant son temps libre?		*What does your friend do in his/her free time?*
Où vas-tu le week-end?		*Where do you go at the weekend?*

Quand j'ai le temps *When I have time*	**je joue** *I play* **mon amie Marie joue** *my friend Marie plays*	**au basket** *basketball* **au foot** *football* **au tennis** *tennis* **aux cartes** *cards* **aux échecs** *chess* **avec mes amis** *with my friends* **avec ses amis** *with her friends*
Quand le ciel est dégagé *When the sky is clear*		
Quand il y a des nuages *When it is cloudy*		
Quand il fait beau *When the weather is good*	**je fais** *I do* **mon ami Lionel fait** *my friend Lionel does*	**du footing** *jogging* **du ski** *skiing* **du sport** *sport* **du vélo** *cycling* **de l'équitation** *horse riding* **de l'escalade** *rock climbing* **de la natation** *swimming* **de la randonnée** *hiking* **mes/ses devoirs** *my/his homework*
Quand il fait mauvais *When the weather is bad*		
Quand il fait chaud *When it is hot*		
Quand il fait froid *When it is cold*		
Quand il y a du soleil *When it is sunny*	**je vais** *I go* **mon amie Anna va** *my friend Anna goes*	**au centre commercial** *to the mall* **au centre sportif** *to the sports centre* **au gymnase** *to the gym* **au parc** *to the park* **à la campagne** *to the countryside* **à la montagne** *to the mountain* **à la pêche** *fishing* **à la piscine** *to the pool* **à la plage** *to the beach* **chez mon ami** *to my friend's house* **chez son ami** *to her friend's house* **en boîte** *clubbing*
Quand il y a du vent *When it is windy*		
Quand il y a du brouillard *When it is foggy*		
Quand il y a de l'orage *When it is stormy*		
Quand il pleut *When it rains*		
Quand il neige *When it snows*		
Parfois *Sometimes*	**je reste** *I stay* **mon ami Philippe reste** *my friend Philippe stays*	**chez moi** *at my home* **dans ma chambre** *in my room* **chez lui** *at his home* **dans sa chambre** *in his room*
Pendant la semaine *During the week*		
Le week-end *At the weekend*		

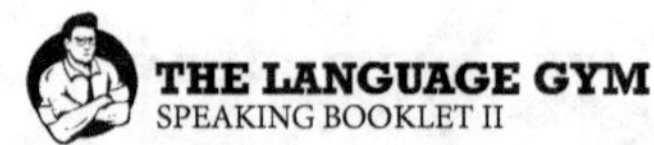

UNIT 1 – FIND SOMEONE WHO – Student Cards

Parfois, je joue aux échecs. **RACHEL**	Pendant la semaine, mon ami fait du ski. **JULES**	Le week-end, je vais au parc. **MARINA**	Quand il fait beau, je joue au foot. **LOUIS**
Quand le ciel est dégagé, mon ami va à la pêche. **VÉRONIQUE**	Quand il fait mauvais, je reste à la maison. **BENOÎT**	Parfois, je joue au basket avec mon frère. **OLIVIA**	Quand j'ai le temps, je vais au centre commercial. **PATRICIA**
Quand il neige, mon amie va au centre sportif. **ROSANNE**	Pendant la semaine, je fais de la randonnée. **MARIE**	Quand il fait chaud, je fais de la natation. **PIERRE**	Quand il y a des nuages, je joue au tennis. **ELSA**
Quand il neige, mon ami fait du ski. **DENIS**	Le week-end, je vais en boîte. **CHARLES**	Quand il fait mauvais, je reste dans ma chambre. **PAUL**	Parfois, je joue au basket. **DAVID**

UNIT 1 – FIND SOMEONE WHO – Student Grid

Que fais-tu pendant ton temps libre?	*What do you do in your free time?*	
Find someone who...		**Name(s)**
1.	...plays football.	
2.	...goes clubbing at weekends.	
3.	...doesn't go out when the weather is bad.	
4.	...has a friend who goes fishing.	
5.	...sometimes plays basketball.	
6.	...goes shopping when they have time.	
7.	...sometimes plays chess.	
8.	...goes to the park at the weekend.	
9.	...plays tennis when it's cloudy.	
10.	...goes swimming when it's hot.	
11.	...has a friend who does skiing.	
12.	...does hiking during the week.	
13.	...has a friend who goes to the sports centre when it's snowing.	

UNIT 1 – ORAL PING-PONG – Person A

ENGLISH	FRENCH
When the weather is bad, my friend (f) plays cards.	Quand il fait mauvais, mon amie joue aux cartes.
When it snows, I go skiing.	
When the weather is good, I go horse riding.	Quand il fait beau, je fais de l'équitation.
When it's windy, I go to the mall.	
When it is stormy, I stay at home.	Quand il y a de l'orage, je reste à la maison.
During the week, I play with my friends.	
When the sky is clear, I go to the gym.	Quand le ciel est dégagé, je vais au gymnase.
When it's sunny, my friend (f) goes fishing.	
At the weekend, my friend (m) goes to the beach.	Le week-end, mon ami va à la plage.
When it's hot, Philippe stays in his room.	

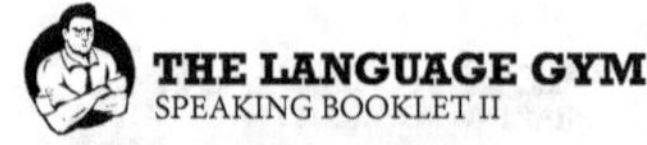

UNIT 1 – ORAL PING-PONG – Person B

ENGLISH	FRENCH
When the weather is bad, my friend (f) plays cards.	
When it snows, I go skiing.	Quand il neige, je fais du ski.
When the weather is good, I go horse riding.	
When it's windy, I go to the mall.	Quand il y a du vent, je vais au centre commercial.
When it is stormy, I stay at home.	
During the week, I play with my friends.	Pendant la semaine, je joue avec mes amis.
When the sky is clear, I go to the gym.	
When it's sunny, my friend (f) goes fishing.	Quand il y a du soleil, mon ami va à la pêche.
At the weekend, my friend (m) goes to the beach.	
When it's hot, Philippe stays in his room.	Quand il fait chaud, Philippe reste dans sa chambre.

No Snakes No Ladders

START

1 — When it's cold, my friend (m) goes skiing.

2 — When it's cloudy, I go swimming.

3 — When I have time, I play football.

4 — When it snows, my friend (m) plays with his friends.

5 — When it's foggy, my friend (f) plays cards.

6 — When it's sunny, I play tennis.

7 — When it's cloudy, my friend (m) plays cards.

8 — When it's windy, my friend (m) does homework.

9 — When it rains, I play chess.

10 — At the weekend, my friend (f) does sport.

11 — When the sky is clear, I go to the beach.

12 — When it's sunny, my friend (f) goes fishing.

13 — When the weather is good, I go to my friend's (m) house.

14 — When the weather is bad, my friend (f) goes to the gym.

15 — When it's windy, my friend (m) rides a bike.

16 — When it's hot, I go to the countryside.

17 — During the week, I stay at home.

18 — At the weekend, I go to the shopping mall.

19 — Sometimes, my friend (m) stays at home.

20 — When I have time, I play basketball.

21 — At the weekend, my friend (m) goes to the beach.

22 — When it snows, I go hiking.

23 — When it's stormy, my friend stays in his room.

24 — Sometimes, my friend (m) goes rock climbing.

25 — When the weather is bad, my friend (m) stays at home.

26 — At the weekend, I go cycling.

27 — When I have time, I play football.

28 — During the week, I go to the gym.

29 — When the sky is clear, I play tennis.

30 — When it rains, I go to the sports centre.

FINISH

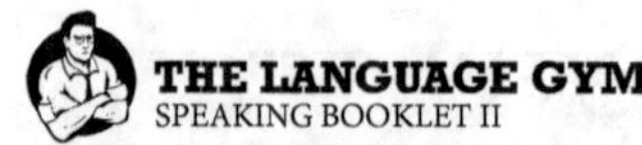

No Snakes No Ladders

	1	2	3	4	5	6	7
DÉPART	Quand il fait froid, mon ami fait du ski.	Quand il y a des nuages, je fais de la natation.	Quand j'ai le temps, je joue au foot.	Quand il neige, mon ami joue avec ses amis.	Quand il y a du brouillard, mon amie joue aux cartes.	Quand il y a du soleil, je joue au tennis.	Quand il y a des nuages, mon ami joue aux cartes.
15 Quand il y a du vent, mon ami fait du vélo.	**14** Quand il fait mauvais, mon amie va au gymnase.	**13** Quand il fait beau, je vais chez mon ami.	**12** Quand il y a du soleil, mon amie va à la pêche.	**11** Quand le ciel est dégagé, je vais à la plage.	**10** Le week-end, mon amie fait du sport.	**9** Quand il pleut, je joue aux échecs.	**8** Quand il y a du vent, mon ami fait ses devoirs.
16 Quand il fait chaud, je vais à la campagne.	**17** Pendant la semaine, je reste à la maison.	**18** Le week-end, je vais au centre commercial.	**19** Parfois, mon ami reste à la maison.	**20** Quand j'ai le temps, je joue au basket.	**21** Le week-end, mon ami va à la plage.	**22** Quand il neige, je fais de la randonnée.	**23** Quand il y a de l'orage, mon ami reste dans sa chambre.
ARRIVÉE	**30** Quand il pleut, je vais au centre sportif.	**29** Quand le ciel est dégagé, je joue au tennis.	**28** Pendant la semaine, je vais au gymnase.	**27** Quand j'ai le temps, je joue au foot.	**26** Le week-end, je fais du vélo.	**25** Quand il fait mauvais, mon ami reste à la maison.	**24** Parfois, mon ami fait de l'escalade.

# UNIT 1 – STAIRCASE TRANSLATION

At the weekend

At the weekend, I play basketball.

At the weekend, I play basketball. During the week, my friend (m) goes to the mall

At the weekend, I play basketball. During the week, my friend (m) goes to the mall. When it rains, I stay at home.

At the weekend, I play basketball. During the week, my friend (m) goes to the mall. When it rains, I stay at home. However (cependant), when it's sunny I do hiking.

At the weekend, I play basketball. During the week, my friend (m) goes to the mall. When it rains, I stay at home. However (cependant), when it's sunny I do hiking. What do you do in your free time?

Translate the final step here:

UNIT 1 – FASTER! 

Say:

1. What do you do in your free time?

2. When I have time, I go to the gym.

3. During the week, I do my homework.

4. What do you do when the weather is bad?

5. When the weather is bad, I stay at home.

6. When it's sunny, I play tennis.

7. What do you do when it snows?

8. When it snows, I do skiing.

9. What does your friend do at the weekend?

10. At the weekend, my friend goes to the mall.

	Time	Mistakes	Referee's name
1			
2			
3			
4			

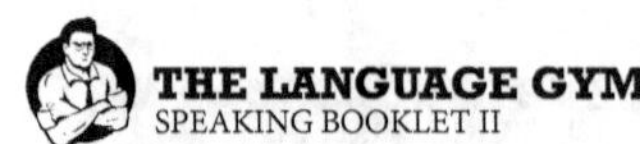

UNIT 1 – FAST & FURIOUS – ROUND 1

1. Le week-end, je __________ chez __________ ami.
   At the weekend, I go to my friend's house.

2. __________ il fait __________ , mon ami va à la plage.
   When the weather is good, my friend goes to the beach.

3. Pendant la semaine, je __________ mes devoirs dans ma __________________ .
   During the week, I do my homework in my room.

4. Quand __________ le temps, je __________ au centre sportif avec ______ amis.
   When I have time, I go to the sports centre with my friends.

5. Quand il y a du __________ , je joue au tennis dans le __________ .
   When it's sunny, I play tennis in the park.

	Time 1	Time 2	Time 3	Time 4
Time				
Mistakes				

UNIT 1 – FAST & FURIOUS – ROUND 2

1. __________ il fait froid, mon amie Olivia ______ à la montagne.
   When it's cold, my friend Olivia goes to the mountain.

2. Le ______________ , je fais du ____________ à la plage.
   At the weekend, I do jogging on the beach.

3. Quand il __________ , je __________ chez moi et je fais ______ devoirs.
   When it rains, I stay at my home and I do my homework.

4. Parfois, mon ____________ va ______ gymnase et il fait du __________ .
   Sometimes, my friend (m) goes to the gym and he does sport.

5. __________ la semaine, __________ le ciel est dégagé, je fais du ________ .
   During the week, when the sky is clear, I go on a bike ride.

	Time 1	Time 2	Time 3	Time 4
Time				
Mistakes				

UNIT 1 – COMMUNICATIVE DRILLS

1	2	3
What do you do when it's cloudy? - When it's cloudy, I play chess with my friends. And you? **Sometimes, I stay at home when it's cloudy.** - Very good.	**What do you do in your free time?** - When I have time, I play tennis with my friends. **I also play tennis at the weekend.** - Great! I like tennis.	**What do you do when the weather is bad?** - I stay at home and do homework. **When the weather is bad, I go to my friend's house.**

4	5	6
What do you do when it's sunny? - When it's sunny, I go to the beach. And you? What do you do when it's sunny? **I really like the beach, but when the weather is good, I go to the park.**	**What does your friend Elsa do when the weather is good?** - When the weather is good, my friend Elsa goes fishing. Do you go fishing? **No, when the weather is good, I play football.** - That's very good!	**Where do you go at the weekend?** - At the weekend, I go to the mall with my family. **That's cool! And during the week?** - During the week, I do sport.

7	8	9
Where do you go during the week? - During the week, I go to the gym with my friend Pierre. And you? What do you do during the week? **During the week, I play basketball at the sports centre.**	**Where does your friend Alain go when the weather is bad?** - My friend Alain stays at home when the weather is bad. And you? **Me too. When the weather is bad, I stay in my house.**	**What do you do at the weekend?** - At the weekend, I play football with my friends. **Very good! I love football.**

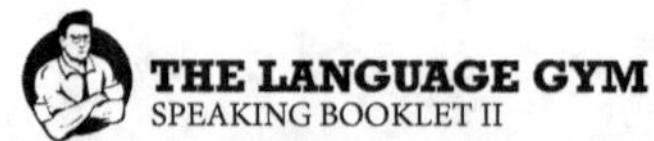

UNIT 1 – COMMUNICATIVE DRILLS
REFEREE CARD

1	2	3
Que fais-tu quand il y a des nuages? - Quand il y a des nuages, je joue aux échecs avec mes amis. Et toi? **Parfois, je reste à la maison quand il y a des nuages.** - Très bien.	**Que fais-tu pendant ton temps libre?** - Quand j'ai le temps, je joue au tennis avec mes amis. **Je joue aussi au tennis le week-end.** - Génial! J'aime le tennis.	**Que fais-tu quand il fait mauvais?** - Je reste chez moi et je fais mes devoirs. **Quand il fait mauvais, je vais chez mon ami(e).**

4	5	6
Que fais-tu quand il y a du soleil? - Quand il y a du soleil, je vais à la plage. Et toi? Que fais-tu quand il y a du soleil? **J'aime beaucoup la plage, mais quand il fait beau, je vais au parc.**	**Que fait ton amie Elsa quand il fait beau?** - Quand il fait beau, mon amie Elsa va à la pêche. Tu vas à la pêche? **Non, quand il fait beau, je joue au foot.** - C'est très bien!	**Où vas-tu le week-end?** - Le week-end, je vais au centre commercial avec ma famille. **C'est cool! Et pendant la semaine?** - Pendant la semaine, je fais du sport.

7	8	9
Où vas-tu pendant la semaine? - Pendant la semaine, je vais au gymnase avec mon ami Pierre. Et toi? Que fais-tu pendant la semaine? **Pendant la semaine, je joue au basket au centre sportif.**	**Où va ton ami Alain quand il fait mauvais?** - Mon ami Alain reste chez lui quand il fait mauvais. Et toi? **Moi aussi. Quand il fait mauvais, je reste chez moi.**	**Que fais-tu le week-end?** - Le week-end, je joue au foot avec mes amis. **Très bien! J'adore le foot.**

UNIT 1 – SURVEY

	Comment tu t'appelles? *What is your name?*	**Que fais-tu pendant ton temps libre?** *What do you do in your free time?*	**Que fais-tu quand il y a du soleil?** *What do you do when it's sunny?*	**Que fais-tu le week-end?** *What do you do at the weekend?*
e.g.	*Je m'appelle Jean.*	*Quand j'ai le temps, je vais au gymnase.*	*Quand il y a du soleil, je vais à la plage.*	*Le week-end, je vais au centre commercial.*
1.				
2.				
3.				
4.				
5.				
6.				
7.				
8.				
9.				

UNIT 1 – ANSWERS

FIND SOMEONE WHO

	Find someone who…	Name(s)
1.	…plays football.	Louis
2.	…goes clubbing at weekends.	Charles
3.	…doesn't like to go out when the weather is bad.	Benoît/Paul
4.	…has a friend who goes fishing.	Véronique
5.	…sometimes plays basketball.	Olivia/David
6.	…goes shopping when they have time.	Patricia
7.	…sometimes plays chess.	Rachel
8.	…goes to the park at the weekend.	Marina
9.	…plays tennis when its cloudy.	Elsa
10.	…goes swimming when it's hot.	Pierre
11.	…has a friend who does skiing.	Jules/Denis
12.	…does hiking during the week.	Marie
13.	…has a friend who goes to the sports centre when it's snowing.	Rosanne

STAIRCASE TRANSLATION

Le week-end, je joue au basket. Pendant la semaine, mon ami va au centre commercial. Quand il pleut, je reste chez moi. Cependant, quand il y a du soleil, je fais de la randonnée. Que fais-tu pendant ton temps libre?

FASTER!

REFEREE SOLUTION

1. Que fais-tu pendant ton temps libre?   2. Quand j'ai le temps, je vais au gymnase.
3. Pendant la semaine, je fais mes devoirs.   4. Que fais-tu quand il fait mauvais?
5. Quand il fait mauvais, je reste chez moi.   6. Quand il y a du soleil, je joue au tennis.
7. Que fais-tu quand il neige?   8. Quand il neige, je fais du ski.   9. Que fait ton ami(e) le week-end?
10. Le week-end, mon ami(e) va au centre commercial.

FAST & FURIOUS

ROUND 1

1. Le week-end, je **vais** chez **mon** ami.
2. **Quand** il fait **beau**, mon ami va à la plage.
3. Pendant la semaine, je **fais** mes devoirs dans ma **chambre**.
4. Quand **j'ai** le temps, je **vais** au centre sportif avec **mes** amis.
5. Quand il y a du **soleil**, je joue au tennis dans le **parc**.

ROUND 2

1. **Quand** il fait froid, mon amie Olivia **va** à la montagne.
2. Le **week-end**, je fais du **footing** à la plage.
3. Quand il **pleut**, je **reste** chez moi et je fais **mes** devoirs.
4. Parfois, mon **ami** va **au** gymnase et il fait du **sport**.
5. **Pendant** la semaine, **quand** le ciel est dégagé, je fais du **vélo**.

UNIT 2.
Talking about my daily routine & activities

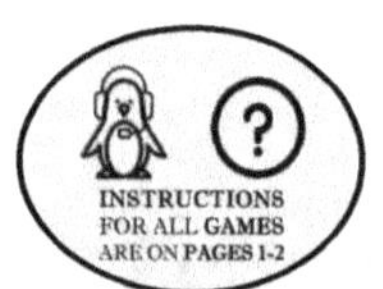

À quelle heure tu te lèves pendant la semaine?	*What time do you get up during the week?*
Que fais-tu avant le collège?	*What do you do before school?*
Que fais-tu quand tu rentres à la maison?	*What do you do when you go back home?*
Que fais-tu pour aider à la maison?	*What do you do to help at home?*

Pendant la semaine *During the week*	**je me brosse les dents** *I brush my teeth*			**une heure**	
	je me couche	*I go to bed*			
	je me douche	*I shower*		**deux**	
	je m'habille	*I get dressed*			
	je me lève	*I get up*		**trois**	
	je me peigne	*I comb my hair*			
	je me repose	*I rest*		**quatre**	**et quart** *quarter past*
Avant le collège *Before school*	**je déjeune**	*I have lunch*		**cinq**	
	je dîne	*I have dinner*	**à**	**six**	
	je fais mes devoirs	*I do my homework*			**et demie** *half past*
	je joue aux jeux vidéo	*I play video games*		**sept** **heures**	
Le matin *In the morning*	**je lis un livre**	*I read a book*			
	je mange des céréales	*I eat cereal*		**huit**	
	je mets mon uniforme *I put on my uniform*			**neuf**	**moins le quart** *quarter to*
L'après-midi *In the afternoon*	**je prends le petit-déjeuner** *I have breakfast*			**dix**	
	je prépare mon sac	*I prepare my bag*		**onze**	
Le soir *In the evening*	**je regarde la télé**	*I watch TV*			
	je rentre à la maison	*I go back home*			
	je sors de chez moi	*I get out of my house*		**midi**	
	je vais au collège	*I go to school*	**à**	**minuit**	
	je vais sur internet	*I go on the internet*			

mais *but*	**aujourd'hui** *today*	**je (ne) dois (pas)** *I -don't- have to*	**aider à la maison**	*help at home*
		je (ne) peux (pas) *I can -not-*	**aller au collège**	*go to school*
			faire les tâches ménagères	*do the chores*
		je (ne) vais (pas) *I am -not- going to*	**faire mes devoirs**	*do my homework*
cependant *however*			**faire mon lit**	*make my bed*
		je (ne) veux (pas) *I -don't- want to*	**me lever tôt**	*wake up early*
			sortir avec mes amis	*go out with my friends*

Author's notes:

1) The verbs *devoir/pouvoir/vouloir* fall into a special category known as "modal verbs". These are used to say what you "have to", "can", or "want" to do.

2) The activities have been arranged by reflexives and non-reflexives. They are organised alphabetically for ease of use. This means that "je me brosse les dents" is first on the list...

UNIT 2 – FIND SOMEONE WHO – Student Cards

Pendant la semaine, je me lève à six heures. **PIERRE**	L'après-midi, je fais mes devoirs à quatre heures et demie. **JEAN**	Pendant la semaine, pour le petit-déjeuner, je mange des céréales à sept heures. **JULIE**	Cet après-midi, je vais aider à la maison et je vais faire mon lit. **MICHEL**
Le matin, je me douche à sept heures et quart. **ALEXANDRA**	Le matin, je sors de chez moi à huit heures. **MARC**	Je déjeune à midi. **PHILIPPE**	Je me douche toujours à sept heures et quart. **OLIVIA**
Avant le collège, je mets mon uniforme à sept heures moins le quart. **PAUL**	Le matin, je m'habille à onze heures et quart. **RAPHAËL**	Pendant la semaine, je me lève à six heures. **ÉRIC**	Cet après-midi, je peux sortir avec mes amies. **AURÉLIE**
Pendant la semaine, je vais au collège à huit heures moins le quart. **SIMON**	Je crois que je dois aider à la maison. **MARIE**	Cet après-midi, je vais sortir avec mon ami. **CAROLINE**	Aujourd'hui, je dois aider à la maison. **LOUIS**

UNIT 2 – FIND SOMEONE WHO – Student Grid

Que fais-tu avant/après le collège?	*What do you do before/after school?*	
Find someone who...		**Name(s)**
1.	...does their homework in the afternoon.	
2.	...leaves home at 8:00 in the morning.	
3.	...can go out with their friends this afternoon.	
4.	...must help at home.	
5.	...gets up at 6:00 during the week.	
6.	...is going to make their bed.	
7.	...has lunch at midday.	
8.	...showers at 7:15 in the morning.	
9.	...goes to school at 7:45 in the morning.	
10.	...eats breakfast at 7:00 in the morning.	
11.	...is going to go out with a friend this afternoon.	
12.	...gets dressed late in the morning.	
13.	...puts on their uniform at 6:45.	

UNIT 2 – ORAL PING-PONG – Person A

ENGLISH	FRENCH
In the morning, I get up at 6:00.	
In the afternoon, I do my homework at 4:00.	L'après-midi, je fais mes devoirs à quatre heures.
Before school, I put on my uniform at 7:00.	.
However, this afternoon, I have to help at home.	Cependant, cet après-midi, je dois aider à la maison.
In the evening, I watch television at 8:30.	
What do you do before school?	Que fais-tu avant le collège?
During the week, I go on the internet at 3:00 p.m.	
In the evening, I read a book, but today, I want to go out with my friend.	Le soir, je lis un livre, mais aujourd'hui, je veux sortir avec mon ami.
What time do you get up during the week?	
In the morning, I have cereal for breakfast.	Le matin, je prends des céréales pour le petit-déjeuner.

UNIT 2 – ORAL PING-PONG – Person B

ENGLISH	FRENCH
In the morning, I get up at 6:00.	Le matin, je me lève à six heures.
In the afternoon, I do my homework at 4:00.	
Before school, I put on my uniform at 7:00.	Avant le collège, je mets mon uniforme à sept heures.
However, this afternoon, I have to help at home.	
In the evening, I watch television at 8:30.	Le soir, je regarde la télé à huit heures et demie.
What do you do before school?	
During the week, I go on the internet at 3:00 p.m.	Pendant la semaine, je vais sur internet à trois heures de l'après-midi.
In the evening, I read a book, but today, I want to go out with my friend.	
What time do you get up during the week?	À quelle heure tu te lèves pendant la semaine?
In the morning, I have cereal for breakfast.	.

No Snakes No Ladders

START

1	In the afternoon, I go out with my friends at 5:00.
2	In the evening, I watch TV at 10:00.
3	During the week, I have lunch at midday.
4	In the morning, I go to school at 9:00.
5	In the morning, I have breakfast at 8:00.
6	During the week, I do my homework at 3:30.
7	In the afternoon, I play videogames at 4:00.
8	In the evening, I go to bed at 11:00.
9	Before school, I get dressed at 7:00.
10	In the afternoon, I go back home at 3:00.
11	Today, I have to do my homework.
12	In the evening, I go on the internet at 8:30.
13	In the morning, I read a book at 8:00.
14	Today, I am going to go out with my friend.
15	In the evening, I brush my teeth at 10:00.
16	In the afternoon, I rest at 4:00.
17	In the morning, I get dressed at 6:15.
18	In the afternoon, I rest at 2:00.
19	However, today, I am going to help at home.
20	In the evening, I go to bed at midnight.
21	In the evening, I have dinner at 7:00.
22	In the afternoon, I prepare my bag at 4:00.
23	During the week, I have lunch at 12:00.
24	Before school, I comb my hair and I put on my uniform.
25	In the evening, I play videogames at 9:30.
26	However, today, I have to get up early.
27	In the afternoon, I go back home at 5:00.
28	In the morning, I have cereal for breakfast.
29	In the evening, I go to bed at 11:00.
30	In the evening, I read a book at 9:00, but today, I am going to go out.

FINISH

No Snakes No Ladders

7 L'après-midi, je joue aux jeux vidéo à quatre heures.	**8** Le soir, je me couche à onze heures.	**23** Pendant la semaine, je déjeune à midi.	**24** Avant le collège, je me peigne et je mets mon uniforme.
6 Pendant la semaine, je fais mes devoirs à trois heures et demie.	**9** Avant le collège, je m'habille à sept heures.	**22** L'après-midi, je prépare mon sac à quatre heures.	**25** Le soir, je joue aux jeux vidéo à neuf heures et demie.
5 Le matin, je prends le petit-déjeuner à huit heures.	**10** L'après-midi, je rentre à la maison à trois heures.	**21** Le soir, je dîne à sept heures.	**26** Cependant, aujourd'hui, je dois me lever tôt.
4 Le matin, je vais au collège à neuf heures.	**11** Aujourd'hui, je dois faire mes devoirs.	**20** Le soir, je me couche à minuit.	**27** L'après-midi, je rentre à la maison à cinq heures.
3 Pendant la semaine, je déjeune à midi.	**12** Le soir, je vais sur internet à huit heures et demie.	**19** Cependant, aujourd'hui, je vais aider à la maison.	**28** Le matin, je prends des céréales pour le petit-déjeuner.
2 Le soir, je regarde la télé à dix heures.	**13** Le matin, je lis un livre à huit heures.	**18** L'après-midi, je me repose à deux heures.	**29** Le soir, je me couche à onze heures.
1 L'après-midi, je sors avec mes amis à cinq heures.	**14** Aujourd'hui, je vais sortir avec mon ami(e).	**17** Le matin, je m'habille à six heures et quart.	**30** Le soir, je lis un livre à neuf heures, mais aujourd'hui, je vais sortir.
DÉPART	**15** Le soir, je me brosse les dents à dix heures.	**16** L'après-midi, je me repose à quatre heures.	**ARRIVÉE**

UNIT 2 – STAIRCASE TRANSLATION

In the afternoon

In the afternoon, I go on the internet.

In the afternoon, I go on the internet at 5:30.

In the afternoon, I go on the internet at 5:30, but today, I have to help at home.

In the afternoon, I go on the internet at 5:30, but today, I have to help at home. In the morning, I get dressed at 6:45.

In the afternoon, I go on the internet at 5:30, but today, I have to help at home. In the morning, I get dressed at 6:45. What time do you get up during the week?

Translate the last step here:

 UNIT 2 – FASTER! 

Say:

1. What time do you get up during the week?

2. Before school, I brush my teeth at 7:15.

3. In the morning, I have cereal for breakfast.

4. What do you do before school?

5. In the afternoon, I read a book, but today, I have to go out with a friend.

6. In the morning, I leave the house at 8:30.

7. During the week, I get up at 9:00, but today, I have to get up early.

8. What do you do when you go back home?

9. In the evening, I have dinner at 8:30.

10. Before school, I shower and I put on my uniform.

	Time	Mistakes	Referee's name
1			
2			
3			
4			

UNIT 2 – TRAPDOOR

Avant le collège L'après-midi Le matin Le soir Pendant la semaine	j'aide à la maison je joue aux jeux vidéo je me brosse les dents je me couche je me douche je me lève je me peigne je mets mon uniforme je m'habille je vais sur internet	à	une deux trois quatre cinq six sept huit neuf dix onze	heure(s)	et quart et demie moins le quart	cependant et mais	aujourd'hui cet après-midi	je dois je peux je vais je veux	aider à la maison aller au collège faire les tâches ménagères faire mes devoirs faire mon lit me lever tôt sortir avec mes amis

ROUND 1

1. During the week, I get up at 7:30, but today, I have to get up early.
2. In the morning, I shower at 10:15, and today, I want to help at home.
3. In the evening, I go on the internet at 8:30, but this afternoon, I want to go out with my friends.
4. In the morning, I get dressed at 5:45, and today, I am going to make my bed.
5. Before school, I play videogames at 8:00. However, today, I have to do my homework.
6. In the evening, I help at home. However, this afternoon, I can go out with my friends.
7. During the week, I watch TV at 8:00, but today, I am going to do my homework.

	Time 1	Time 2	Time 3	Time 4
Time				
Mistakes				

ROUND 2

1. In the morning, I have cereal for breakfast at 6:00, and today, I have to help at home.
2. In the afternoon, I play videogames at 5:00. However, this afternoon, I have to do my homework.
3. In the evening, I have dinner at 8:30, and today, I am going to go out with my friend.
4. Before school, I have breakfast at 6:30, and today, I want to make my bed.
5. During the week, I watch television at 5:00, but this afternoon, I am going to do my homework.
6. Before school, I read a book at 6:30, but today, I have to go to school early.
7. In the afternoon, I go back home at 3:45, and today, I want to go out with a friend.

	Time 1	Time 2	Time 3	Time 4
Time				
Mistakes				

UNIT 2 – COMMUNICATIVE DRILLS

1	2	3
What do you do before school? - Before school, I get up and I shower. And you? **In the morning, I get dressed at 7:30 and go to school.** - I also get dressed at 7:30.	**What do you do to help at home?** - In the afternoon, I have to do household chores, and today, I am going to make my bed. **What do you do during the week?** - During the week, I watch TV and I play videogames.	**What do you do when you come back home?** - In the afternoon, I rest at 4:30, but this evening, I am going to do my homework. And you? **In the evening, I read a book and I rest. However, today, I have to help at home.**

4	5	6
At what time do you get up during the week? - During the week, I get up at 7:00. However, today, I want to get up early. **What do you do before school?** - Before school, I have cereal for breakfast at 7:45 and I put on my uniform.	**What do you do during the week?** - During the week, I prepare my bag and I go on the internet. However, this afternoon, I have to do household chores. And you? **Before school, I comb my hair and I get dressed at 6:15, but today, I also have to make my bed.**	**What do you do in the evening?** - In the evening, I play videogames at 8:30. However, this evening, I can go out with my friend. **At what time do you get up during the week?** - During the week, I get up at 5:30. And you? **In the morning, I get up at five!**

7	8	9
What do you do when you come back home? - When I come back home, I go on the internet and I play videogames. **What do you do to help at home?** - I have to do household chores.	**What do you do during the week?** - During the week, I get out of my house at 6:15. However, today, I don't have to go to school. And you? **During the week, I watch TV at quarter to nine, but this evening, I am going to help at home. And you?** - This afternoon, I am going to help at home and I am going to do household chores.	**What do you do in the afternoon?** - In the afternoon, I come back home at 5:00 and I have dinner at 7:00. **What do you do in the evening?** - In the evening, I go to bed at 9:00, but this evening, I am going out with a friend. What do you do in the evening? **In the evening, I go on the internet and I shower.**

UNIT 2 – COMMUNICATIVE DRILLS
REFEREE CARD

1	2	3
Que fais-tu avant le collège? - Avant le collège, je me lève et je me douche. Et toi? **Le matin, je m'habille à sept heures et demie et je vais au collège.** - Je m'habille aussi à sept heures et demie.	**Que fais-tu pour aider à la maison?** - L'après-midi, je dois faire les tâches ménagères et aujourd'hui, je vais faire mon lit. **Que fais-tu pendant la semaine?** - Pendant la semaine, je regarde la télé et je joue aux jeux vidéo.	**Que fais-tu quand tu rentres à la maison?** - L'après-midi, je me repose à quatre heures et demie, mais ce soir, je vais faire mes devoirs. Et toi? **Le soir, je lis un livre et je me repose. Cependant, aujourd'hui, je dois aider à la maison.**

4	5	6
À quelle heure tu te lèves pendant la semaine? - Pendant la semaine, je me lève à sept heures. Cependant, aujourd'hui je veux me lever tôt. **Que fais-tu avant le collège?** - Avant le collège, je prends des céréales pour le petit-déjeuner à huit heures moins le quart et je mets mon uniforme.	**Que fais-tu pendant la semaine?** - Pendant la semaine, je prépare mon sac et je vais sur internet. Cependant, cet après-midi, je dois faire les tâches ménagères. Et toi? **Avant le collège, je me peigne et je m'habille à six heures et quart, mais aujourd'hui, je dois aussi faire mon lit.**	**Que fais-tu le soir?** - Le soir, je joue aux jeux vidéo à huit heures et demie. Cependant, ce soir, je peux sortir avec mon ami(e). **À quelle heure tu te lèves pendant la semaine?** - Pendant la semaine, je me lève à cinq heures et demie. Et toi? **Le matin, je me lève à cinq heures!**

7	8	9
Que fais-tu quand tu rentres à la maison? - Quand je rentre à la maison, je vais sur internet et je joue aux jeux vidéo. **Que fais-tu pour aider à la maison?** - Je dois faire les tâches ménagères.	**Que fais-tu pendant la semaine?** - Pendant la semaine, je sors de chez moi à six heures et quart. Cependant, aujourd'hui, je ne dois pas aller au collège. Et toi? **Pendant la semaine, je regarde la télé à neuf heures moins le quart, mais ce soir, je vais aider à la maison. Et toi?** - Cet après-midi, je vais aider à la maison et je vais faire les tâches ménagères.	**Que fais-tu l'après-midi?** - L'après-midi, je rentre à la maison à cinq heures et je dîne à sept heures. **Que fais-tu le soir?** - Le soir, je me couche à neuf heures, mais ce soir je vais sortir avec un(e) ami(e). Que fais-tu le soir? **Le soir, je vais sur internet et je me douche.**

UNIT 2 – SURVEY

	Comment tu t'appelles? *What is your name?*	À quelle heure tu te lèves pendant la semaine? *What time do you get up during the week?*	Que fais-tu avant le collège? *What do you do before school?*	Que fais-tu l'après-midi? *What do you do in the afternoon?*	Que fais-tu pendant la semaine? *What do you do during the week?*
e.g.	*Je m'appelle Jean.*	*Pendant la semaine, je me lève à six heures moins le quart.*	*Avant le collège, je mets mon uniforme à sept heures.*	*L'après-midi, je joue aux jeux vidéo à cinq heures.*	*Pendant la semaine, je fais mes devoirs à quatre heures et demie.*
1.					
2.					
3.					
4.					
5.					
6.					
7.					

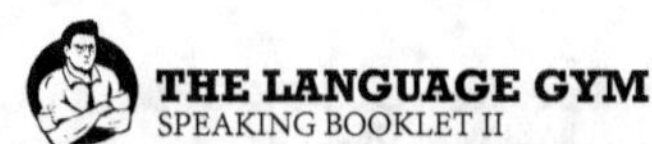

UNIT 2 – ANSWERS

FIND SOMEONE WHO

Find someone who...		Name(s)
1.	...does their homework in the afternoon.	**Jean**
2.	...leaves home at 8:00 in the morning.	**Marc**
3.	...can go out with their friends this afternoon.	**Aurélie**
4.	...must help at home.	**Marie/Louis**
5.	...gets up at 6:00 during the week.	**Pierre/Éric**
6.	...is going to make their bed.	**Michel**
7.	...has lunch at midday.	**Philippe**
8.	...showers at 7:15 in the morning.	**Alexandra/Olivia**
9.	...goes to school at 7:45 in the morning.	**Simon**
10.	...eats breakfast at 7:00 in the morning.	**Julie**
11.	...is going to go out with a friend this afternoon.	**Caroline**
12.	...gets dressed late in the morning.	**Raphaël**
13.	...puts on their uniform at 6:45.	**Paul**

STAIRCASE TRANSLATION

L'après-midi, je vais sur internet à cinq heures et demie, mais aujourd'hui, je dois aider à la maison. Le matin, je m'habille à sept heures moins le quart. À quelle heure tu te lèves pendant la semaine?

FASTER!

REFEREE SOLUTION:

1. À quelle heure tu te lèves pendant la semaine?
2. Avant le collège, je me brosse les dents à sept heures et quart.
3. Le matin, je prends des céréales pour le petit-déjeuner.
4. Que fais-tu avant le collège?
5. L'après-midi, je lis un livre, mais aujourd'hui, je dois sortir avec un ami.
6. Le matin, je sors de chez moi à huit heures et demie.
7. Pendant la semaine, je me lève à neuf heures, mais aujourd'hui, je dois me lever tôt.
8. Que fais-tu quand tu rentres à la maison?
9. Le soir, je dîne à huit heures et demie.
10. Avant le collège, je me douche et je mets mon uniforme.

TRAPDOOR

ROUND 1

1. Pendant la semaine, je me lève à sept heures et demie, mais aujourd'hui, je dois me lever tôt.
2. Le matin, je me douche à dix heures et quart, et aujourd'hui, je veux aider à la maison.
3. Le soir, je vais sur internet à huit heures et demie, mais cet après-midi, je veux sortir avec mes amis.
4. Le matin, je m'habille à six heures moins le quart, et aujourd'hui, je vais faire mon lit.
5. Avant le collège, je joue aux jeux vidéo à huit heures. Cependant, aujourd'hui, je dois faire mes devoirs.
6. Le soir, j'aide à la maison. Cependant, cet après-midi, je peux sortir avec mes amis.
7. Pendant la semaine, je regarde la télé à huit heures, mais aujourd'hui, je vais faire mes devoirs.

ROUND 2

1. Le matin, je prends des céréales pour le petit-déjeuner à six heures, et aujourd'hui, je dois aider à la maison.
2. L'après-midi, je joue aux jeux vidéo à cinq heures. Cependant cet après-midi, je dois faire mes devoirs.
3. Le soir, je dîne à huit heures et demie et aujourd'hui, je vais sortir avec mon ami(e).
4. Avant le collège, je prends le petit-déjeuner à six heures et demie et aujourd'hui, je veux faire mon lit.
5. Pendant la semaine, je regarde la télé à cinq heures, mais cet après-midi, je vais faire mes devoirs.
6. Avant le collège, je lis un livre à six heures et demie, mais aujourd'hui je dois aller au collège tôt.
7. L'après-midi, je rentre à la maison à quatre heures moins le quart et aujourd'hui, je veux sortir avec un ami.

UNIT 3.
Saying what I do at home

Que fais-tu pendant ton temps libre?	*What do you do in your free time?*
Que fais-tu dans ta chambre?	*What do you do in your bedroom?*
Combien de fois par semaine?	*How many times a week?*
Où fais-tu cela?	*Where do you do this?*

D'habitude *Usually*	**je discute avec ma mère**	*I chat with my mum*		**la chambre de mon frère** *my brother's bedroom*
De temps en temps *From time to time*	**j'écoute de la musique**	*I listen to music*		**la chambre de mes parents** *my parents' bedroom*
Deux fois par semaine *Twice a week*	**je fais du vélo**	*I ride my bike*		**ma chambre** *my bedroom*
Généralement *Generally*	**je fais mes devoirs**	*I do my homework*		**la cuisine** *the kitchen*
Normalement *Normally*	**je joue à la PlayStation**	*I play PlayStation*		**le garage** *the garage*
Parfois *Sometimes*	**je lis des bandes dessinées**	*I read comics*	**dans** *in*	**le jardin** *the garden*
Quand j'ai le temps *When I have time*	**je lis des magazines**	*I read magazines*		**la salle de bains** *the bathroom*
Souvent *Often*	**je lis des romans**	*I read novels*		**la salle de jeux** *the game room*
Tous les jours *Every day*	**je me brosse les dents**	*I brush my teeth*		**la salle à manger** *the dining room*
Trois fois par mois *Three times a month*	**je me douche**	*I shower*		**le salon** *the living room*
Vers six, sept, huit... heures du matin *At around 6, 7, 8am...*	**je m'habille**	*I get dressed*		
	je me lave	*I have a wash*		
	je me repose	*I rest*		
	je prends le petit-déjeuner	*I have breakfast*		
	je prépare le repas	*I prepare food*		
	je poste des photos sur Instagram *I post photos on Instagram*			
	je regarde la télé	*I watch TV*		
	je regarde des films	*I watch films*		
	je regarde des séries sur Netflix *I watch a series on Netflix*			
	je sors de chez moi	*I leave the house*		
	je surfe/vais sur internet	*I surf/go on the internet*	**sur la terrasse** *on the terrace*	

***Author's note:** In this unit, you will come across the words "always" *(toujours)* and "never" *(jamais)*.
Here's how to use them in a sentence:
-**"Toujours"** is placed after the verb in a sentence.
e.g: Je regarde toujours des séries sur Netflix   *I always watch series on Netflix*
-**"Jamais"** works on the same model as the negative *ne... (verb) pas* in a sentence: *ne... (verb) jamais.*
e.g: Je **ne** regarde **jamais** la télé   *I never watch TV*

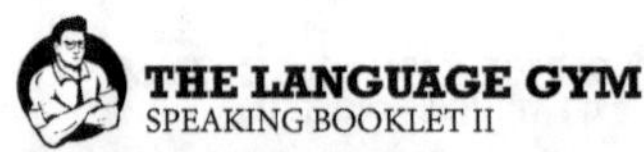

UNIT 3 – FIND SOMEONE WHO – Student Cards

Vers six heures du matin, je prends le petit-déjeuner dans la cuisine. **PIERRE**	En général, je regarde des séries sur Netflix dans la salle de jeux. **JEAN**	Tous les jours, je me repose dans la salle à manger. **JULIE**	Souvent, je prépare le repas dans la cuisine. **SÉBASTIEN**
Deux fois par semaine, je joue à la PlayStation dans le salon. **NINON**	Souvent, je lis des magazines sur la terrasse. **MARIE**	Parfois, je fais du vélo dans le jardin. **PAUL**	Quand j'ai le temps, je poste des photos sur Instagram. **ALEXANDRE**
Quand j'ai le temps, je discute avec ma mère dans le jardin. **JULIEN**	Quand j'ai le temps, je vais sur internet dans ma chambre. **DANIEL**	En général, je regarde des films dans la salle de jeux. **AMÉLIE**	Je ne regarde jamais la télé dans le garage. **CATHERINE**
Je lis toujours des magazines sur la terrasse. **PHILIPPE**	Le matin, je prends le petit-déjeuner dans la cuisine vers six heures. **MARTINE**	Je fais toujours du vélo dans le jardin avec mes frères. **GEORGES**	Tous les jours, je regarde la télé dans le salon. **DAVID**

UNIT 3 – FIND SOMEONE WHO – Student Grid

	Que fais-tu pendant ton libre? *What do you do in your free time?*	
	Find someone who...	**Name(s)**
1.	...rests every day in the dining room.	
2.	...plays on the PlayStation in the living room.	
3.	...watches television in the living room.	
4.	...reads magazines on the terrace.	
5.	...posts photos on Instagram.	
6.	...usually watches films in the games room.	
7.	...rides their bike.	
8.	...often prepares food in the kitchen.	
9.	...has breakfast in the kitchen at around 6:00 a.m.	
10.	...always goes on the internet in their bedroom.	
11.	...always chats with their mother in the garden.	
12.	...usually watches series on Netflix in the games room.	
13.	...never watches television in the garage.	

UNIT 3 – ORAL PING-PONG – Person A

ENGLISH	FRENCH	ENGLISH	FRENCH
What do you do in your free time?	Que fais-tu pendant ton temps libre?	**At around 6:00 a.m., I get dressed in my bedroom.**	Vers six heures du matin, je m'habille dans ma chambre.
At around 6:00 a.m., I have breakfast in the kitchen.		**Twice a week, I prepare food in the kitchen.**	
I always chat with my mum in my parents' bedroom.	Je discute toujours avec ma mère dans la chambre de mes parents.	**Sometimes, I watch a series on Netflix in the living room.**	Parfois, je regarde des séries sur Netflix dans le salon.
Every day, I watch television in the dining room.		**I always do my homework in the games room.**	
Sometimes, I ride my bike in the garden.	Parfois, je fais du vélo dans le jardin.	**When I have time, I read comics in the garage.**	Quand j'ai le temps, je lis des bandes dessinées dans le garage.
I never watch films in the living room.		**What do you do in your bedroom?**	
Twice a week, I play on the PlayStation in the games room.	Deux fois par semaine, je joue à la PlayStation dans la salle de jeux.	**Often, I read magazines on the terrace.**	Souvent, je lis des magazines sur la terrasse.
Often, I listen to music on the terrace.		**I never go on the internet in the garage.**	
When I have time, I post photos on Instagram.	Quand j'ai le temps, je poste des photos sur Instagram.	**Usually, I chat on WhatsApp in the dining room.**	D'habitude, je discute sur WhatsApp dans la salle à manger.
Usually, I rest in my brother's bedroom.		**I always have breakfast on the terrace.**	

UNIT 3 – ORAL PING-PONG – Person B

ENGLISH	FRENCH	ENGLISH	FRENCH
What do you do in your free time?		At around 6:00 a.m., I get dressed in my bedroom.	
At around 6:00 a.m., I have breakfast in the kitchen.	Vers six heures du matin, je prends le petit-déjeuner dans la cuisine.	Twice a week, I prepare food in the kitchen.	Deux fois par semaine, je prépare le repas dans la cuisine.
I always chat with my mum in my parents' bedroom.		Sometimes, I watch a series on Netflix in the living room.	
Every day, I watch television in the dining room.	Tous les jours, je regarde la télé dans la salle à manger.	I always do my homework in the games room.	Je fais toujours mes devoirs dans la salle de jeux.
Sometimes, I ride my bike in the garden.		When I have time, I read comics in the garage.	
I never watch films in the living room.	Je ne regarde jamais de films dans le salon.	What do you do in your bedroom?	Que fais-tu dans ta chambre?
Twice a week, I play on the PlayStation in the games room.		Often, I read magazines on the terrace.	
Often, I listen to music on the terrace.	Souvent, j'écoute de la musique sur la terrasse.	I never go on the internet in the garage.	Je ne vais jamais sur internet dans le garage.
When I have time, I post photos on Instagram.		Usually, I chat on WhatsApp in the dining room.	
Usually, I rest in my brother's bedroom.	D'habitude, je me repose dans la chambre de mon frère.	I always have breakfast on the terrace.	Je prends toujours le petit-déjeuner sur la terrasse.

No Snakes No Ladders

START

1 — I always go on the internet in the living room.

2 — Often, I read comics in my bedroom.

3 — Usually, I watch TV in the dining room.

4 — When I have time, I post photos on Instagram.

5 — Sometimes, I rest in the garden.

6 — Every day, I play on the PlayStation in the games room.

7 — At around 6:00 a.m., I brush my teeth in the bathroom.

8 — What do you do in your free time?

9 — I never play on the PlayStation in the garage.

10 — When I have time, I watch movies in the living room.

11 — I never chat on WhatsApp in the living room.

12 — Usually, I have breakfast in the kitchen.

13 — I always watch series on Netflix in my bedroom.

14 — Sometimes, I ride my bike in the garden.

15 — Twice a week, I post photos on Instagram.

16 — Every day, I shower in the bathroom.

17 — How many times a week?

18 — Sometimes, I rest in the games room.

19 — Usually, I watch TV in the living room.

20 — I always brush my teeth in the bathroom.

21 — Every day, I listen to music in the garden.

22 — Often, I get dressed in my bedroom.

23 — When I have time, I prepare food in the kitchen.

24 — At around 6:00 a.m., I have breakfast in the kitchen.

25 — I always go on the internet in my bedroom.

26 — Often, I watch TV in my parents' bedroom.

27 — Every day, I read magazines in the games room.

28 — Twice a week, I chat with my mum in the garden.

29 — Sometimes, I watch a series on Netflix in the living room.

30 — When I have time, I brush my teeth in the bathroom.

FINISH

No Snakes No Ladders

DÉPART

1. Je vais toujours sur internet dans le salon.
2. Souvent, je lis des bandes dessinées dans ma chambre.
3. D'habitude, je regarde la télé dans la salle à manger.
4. Quand j'ai le temps, je poste des photos sur Instagram.
5. Parfois, je me repose dans le jardin.
6. Tous les jours, je joue à la PlayStation dans la salle de jeux.
7. Vers six heures du matin, je me brosse les dents dans la salle de bains.
8. Que fais-tu pendant ton temps libre?
9. Je ne joue jamais à la PlayStation dans le garage.
10. Quand j'ai le temps, je regarde des films dans le salon.
11. Je ne discuste jamais sur WhatsApp dans le salon.
12. D'habitude, je prends le petit-déjeuner dans la cuisine.
13. Je regarde toujours des séries sur Netflix dans ma chambre.
14. Parfois, je fais du vélo dans le jardin.
15. Deux fois par semaine, je poste des photos sur Instagram.
16. Tous les jours, je me douche dans la salle de bains.
17. Combien de fois par semaine?
18. Parfois, je me repose dans la salle de jeux.
19. D'habitude, je regarde la télé dans le salon.
20. Je me brosse toujours les dents dans la salle de bains.
21. Tous les jours, j'écoute de la musique dans le jardin.
22. Souvent, je m'habille dans ma chambre.
23. Quand j'ai le temps, je prépare le repas dans la cuisine.
24. Vers six heures du matin, je prends le petit-déjeuner dans la cuisine.
25. Je vais toujours sur internet dans ma chambre.
26. Souvent, je regarde la télé dans la chambre de mes parents.
27. Tous les jours, je lis des magazines dans la salle de jeux.
28. Deux fois par semaine, je discute avec ma mère dans le jardin.
29. Parfois, je regarde des séries sur Netflix dans le salon.
30. Quand j'ai le temps, je me brosse les dents dans la salle de bains.

ARRIVÉE

UNIT 3 – STAIRCASE TRANSLATION

Every day

Every day, I watch television in the living room.

Every day, I watch television in the living room. When I have time, I listen to music.

Every day, I watch television in the living room. When I have time, I listen to music in my bedroom. Twice a week, I post photos on Instagram.

Every day, I watch television in the living room. When I have time, I listen to music in my bedroom. Twice a week, I post photos on Instagram. I never ride my bike in the garden.

Every day, I watch television in the living room. When I have time, I listen to music in my bedroom. Twice a week, I post photos on Instagram. I never ride my bike in the garden. What do you do in your free time?

Translate the last step here:

 # UNIT 3 – FASTER! 

Say:

1. Often, I listen to music in the garden.

2. When I have time, I watch films in the living room.

3. I never have breakfast in the dining room.

4. Sometimes, I do my homework on the terrace.

5. Usually, I get dressed in my bedroom.

6. I always brush my teeth in the bathroom.

7. Every day, I watch TV in my brother's bedroom.

8. Twice a week, I prepare food in the kitchen.

9. At around 6:00 a.m., I do my homework in the games room.

10. When I have time, I read magazines in my parents' bedroom.

	Time	Mistakes	Referee's name
1			
2			
3			
4			

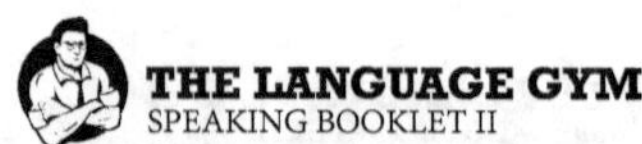

UNIT 3 – INFORMATION GAP TASK

Use these questions to find out the missing information from your partner. Answer the questions in the first person wherever you can: e.g. **"je vais sur internet"**.

Combien de fois par semaine...? *How many times a week...?* **Où...?** *Where...?*	...**tu vas sur internet?** ...**tu lis des magazines?** ...**tu regardes la télé?** ...**tu joues à la PlayStation ?** ...**tu écoutes de la musique?** ...**tu te brosses les dents?** ...**tu prépares le repas?**	*...do you go on the internet?* *...do you read magazines?* *...do you watch TV?* *...do you play on the PlayStation?* *...do you listen to music?* *...do you brush your teeth?* *...do you prepare food?*
Que fais-tu...? *What do you do...?*	...**d'habitude?** ...**parfois?** ...**toujours?** ...**tous les jours?** ...**souvent?** ...**pendant ton temps libre?**	*...usually?* *...sometimes?* *...always?* *...every day?* *...often?* *...in your free time?*

PARTNER 1

	Activity	How often	Location
Joël	**Go on the internet**		**In the living room**
Sandra		**Often**	
Paul	**Listen to music**		**In my bedroom**
Daniel	**Brush teeth**	**Every day**	
Sarah		**Sometimes**	**In the kitchen**

PARTNER 2

	Activity	How often	Location
Joël		**Always**	
Sandra	**Play on the PlayStation**		**In the games room**
Paul		**Usually**	
Daniel			**In the bathroom**
Sarah	**Prepare food**		

UNIT 3 – COMMUNICATIVE DRILLS

1	2	3
What do you do in your free time? - Sometimes, I watch TV in the living room. **How many times a week do you do your homework?** - Every day.	**What do you do in your free time?** - When I have time, I prepare food in the kitchen. **How many times a week do you play on the PlayStation?** - Twice a week, I play on the PlayStation in the games room.	**Where do you brush your teeth?** - Usually, I brush my teeth in the bathroom. And you? **Me too, but sometimes, I brush my teeth in the kitchen.** - Me too!

4	5	6
What do you do in your bedroom? - Often, I rest in my bedroom. When I have time, I read magazines. And you? **I never read magazines in my bedroom.**	**What do you do in your free time?** - I always go on the internet in my brother's bedroom. **How many times a week do you do it?** - I go on the internet every day.	**How many times a week do you prepare food?** - I never prepare food. And you? **I prepare food in the kitchen every day.** - Usually, I have breakfast in the kitchen.

7	8	9
Twice a week, I chat with my mum on the terrace. And you? - I always chat with my mum in the living room. **Where do you read comics?** - I read comics in the garage.	**What do you do in your bedroom?** - Usually, I get dressed and I rest in my bedroom. **What do you do in your free time?** - I always listen to music in the dining room.	**What do you do every day?** - Every day, I watch films in the games room. **Where do you play on the PlayStation?** - Often, I play on the PlayStation in the living room.

UNIT 3 – COMMUNICATIVE DRILLS
REFEREE CARD

1	2	3
Que fais-tu pendant ton temps libre? - Parfois, je regarde la télé dans le salon. **Combien de fois par semaine tu fais tes devoirs?** - Tous les jours.	**Que fais-tu pendant ton temps libre?** - Quand j'ai le temps, je prépare le repas dans la cuisine. **Combien de fois par semaine tu joues à la PlayStation?** - Deux fois par semaine, je joue à la PlayStation dans la salle de jeux.	**Où tu te brosses les dents?** - D'habitude, je me brosse les dents dans la salle de bains. Et toi? **Moi aussi, mais parfois, je me brosse les dents dans la cuisine.** - Moi aussi!
4	**5**	**6**
Que fais-tu dans ta chambre? - Souvent, je me repose dans ma chambre. Quand j'ai le temps, je lis des magazines. Et toi? **Je ne lis jamais de magazines dans ma chambre.**	**Que fais-tu pendant ton temps libre?** - Je vais toujours sur internet dans la chambre de mon frère. **Combien de fois par semaine fais-tu cela?** - Je vais sur internet tous les jours.	**Combien de fois par semaine tu prépares le repas?** - Je ne prépare jamais le repas. Et toi? **Je prépare le repas dans la cuisine tous les jours.** - D'habitude, je prends le petit-déjeuner dans la cuisine.
7	**8**	**9**
Deux fois par semaine, je discute avec ma mère sur la terrasse. Et toi? - Je discute toujours avec ma mère dans le salon. **Où lis-tu des bandes dessinées?** - Je lis des bandes dessinées dans le garage.	**Que fais-tu dans ta chambre?** - D'habitude, je m'habille et je me repose dans ma chambre. **Que fais-tu pendant ton temps libre?** - J'écoute toujours de la musique dans la salle à manger.	**Que fais-tu tous les jours?** - Tous les jours, je regarde des films dans la salle de jeux. **Où tu joues à la PlayStation ?** - Souvent, je joue à la PlayStation dans le salon.

UNIT 3 – SURVEY

	Comment tu t'appelles? *What is your name?*	Que fais-tu pendant ton temps libre? *What do you do in your free time?*	Tu écoutes souvent de la musique? *How often do you listen to music?*	Où fais-tu tes devoirs? *Where do you do homework?*	Que fais-tu dans le salon? *What do you do in the living room?*	Que fais-tu dans la cuisine? *What do you do in the kitchen?*
e.g.	*Je m'appelle Jean.*	*Quand j'ai le temps, je regarde des films dans ma chambre.*	*Deux fois par semaine, j'écoute de la musique sur la terrasse.*	*Souvent, je fais mes devoirs dans la salle à manger.*	*Souvent, je lis des magazines dans le salon.*	*D'habitude, je prends le petit-déjeuner dans la cuisine.*
1.						
2.						
3.						
4.						
5.						
6.						
7.						

UNIT 3 – ANSWERS

FIND SOMEONE WHO

	Find someone who...	Name(s)
1.	...rests every day in the dining room.	**Julie**
2.	...plays on the PlayStation in the living room.	**Ninon**
3.	...watches television in the living room.	**David**
4.	...reads magazines on the terrace.	**Marie/Philippe**
5.	...posts photos on Instagram.	**Alexandre**
6.	...usually watches films in the games room.	**Amélie**
7.	...rides their bike.	**Paul/Georges**
8.	...often prepares food in the kitchen.	**Sébastien**
9.	...has breakfast in the kitchen at around 6:00 a.m.	**Pierre/Martine**
10.	...always goes on the internet in their bedroom.	**Daniel**
11.	...always chats with their mother in the garden.	**Julien**
12.	...usually watches series in the games room.	**Jean**
13.	...never watches television in the garage.	**Catherine**

STAIRCASE TRANSLATION

Tous les jours, je regarde la télé dans le salon. Quand j'ai le temps, j'écoute de la musique dans ma chambre. Deux fois par semaine, je poste des photos sur Instagram. Je ne fais jamais de vélo dans le jardin. Que fais-tu pendant ton temps libre?

FASTER!

REFEREE SOLUTION:
1. Souvent, j'écoute de la musique dans le jardin.
2. Quand j'ai le temps, je regarde des films dans le salon.
3. Je ne prends jamais le petit-déjeuner dans la salle à manger.
4. Parfois, je fais mes devoirs sur la terrasse.
5. D'habitude, je m'habille dans ma chambre.
6. Je me brosse toujours les dents dans la salle de bains.
7. Tous les jours, je regarde la télé dans la chambre de mon frère.
8. Deux fois par semaine, je prépare le repas dans la cuisine.
9. Vers six heures du matin, je fais mes devoirs dans la salle de jeux.
10. Quand j'ai le temps, je lis des magazines dans la chambre de mes parents.

INFORMATION GAP TASK

	Activity	How often	Location
Joël	**Go on the internet**	**Always**	**In the living room**
Sandra	**Play on the PlayStation**	**Often**	**In the games room**
Paul	**Listen to music**	**Usually**	**In my bedroom**
Daniel	**Brush teeth**	**Every day**	**In the bathroom**
Sarah	**Prepare food**	**Sometimes**	**In the kitchen**

UNIT 4.
Talking about the clothes I wear

Quels vêtements portes-tu à la maison?	What clothes do you wear at home?
Que portes-tu quand il fait froid/chaud?	What do you wear when it's cold/hot?
Que portes-tu quand tu sors avec tes amis?	What do you wear when you go out with your friends?
Décris ton uniforme scolaire.	Describe your school uniform.

		FEM			
Quand il fait chaud *When it is hot*		une casquette	a baseball cap	**blanche**	white
Quand il fait froid *When it is cold*		une chemise	a shirt	**bleue**	blue
		une ceinture	a belt	**grise**	grey
Quand je sors avec mon ami/amie *When I go out with my friend*		une cravate	a tie	**jaune**	yellow
		une écharpe	a scarf	**marron**	brown
		une jupe	a skirt	**noire**	black
		une montre	a watch	**orange**	orange
		une robe	a dress	**rouge**	red
Quand je sors avec mes amis *When I go out with my friends*	**je porte** *I wear*	une veste	a jacket	**verte**	green
		une veste de sport	a sports jacket		
Quand je joue au foot *When I play football*		MASC			
		un chapeau	a hat		
		un collier	a necklace		
		un costume	a suit	**blanc**	
		un gilet	a waistcoat	**bleu**	
À la maison *At home*		un haut	a top	**gris**	
En discothèque *At the nightclub*		un jean	jeans	**jaune**	
		un maillot de bain	a swimsuit	**marron**	
Au collège *At school*		un manteau	a coat	**noir**	
		un pantalon	trousers	**orange**	
Au gymnase *At the gym*		un pull	jumper	**rouge**	
À la plage *At the beach*	**il/elle porte** *he/she wears*	un short	shorts	**vert**	
		un survêtement	a tracksuit		
		un tee-shirt	a T-shirt		
		un tee-shirt sans manches	tank top / vest		
		un uniforme	a uniform		
		PLURAL FEM			
Normalement *Normally*		des bottes	boots	**blanches**	
En général *In general*		des boucles d'oreilles	earrings	**bleues**	
		des chaussettes	socks	**grises**	
Souvent *Often*		des chaussures	shoes	**jaunes**	
		des chaussures à talons hauts	*high heel shoes*	**marron**	
		des chaussures de sport	sports shoes	**noires**	
		des pantoufles	slippers	**orange**	
		des sandales	sandals	**rouges**	
				vertes	

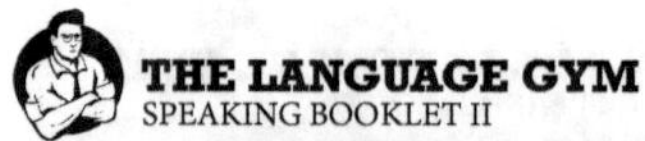
THE LANGUAGE GYM
SPEAKING BOOKLET II

UNIT 4 – FIND SOMEONE WHO – Student Cards

Je porte toujours une casquette rouge. **JULIE**	À la plage, je porte un maillot de bain blanc. **LUCIE**	Au gymnase, je porte des chaussures de sport bleues. **FERNAND**	Quand il fait froid, je porte une écharpe rouge. **AURORE**
Quand je sors avec ma petite amie, je porte un costume bleu. **MICHEL**	À la maison, je porte un short orange. **JEAN**	Au collège, je porte un uniforme marron. **LÉA**	Quand je joue au foot, je porte un short blanc. **MARTINE**
Quand je sors avec mes parents, je porte un pull noir. **LAURE**	Quand il fait froid, je porte un pantalon gris. **HÉLÈNE**	Je ne porte jamais de veste verte. **GEORGES**	En discothèque, je porte une ceinture jaune. **JOËL**
D'habitude, je porte une cravate noire. **CARLA**	Quand il fait froid, je porte une écharpe rouge. **CHARLES**	Quand il fait chaud, je porte un tee-shirt blanc. **ANTHONY**	À la maison, je porte un short orange. **ALICE**

UNIT 4 – FIND SOMEONE WHO – Student Grid

Quels vêtements portes-tu?	*What clothes do you wear?*	
Find someone who...		**Name(s)**
1.	...wears a red scarf when it's cold.	
2.	...wears a white t-shirt when it's hot.	
3.	...wears orange shorts at home.	
4.	...wears white shorts when playing football.	
5.	...wears a blue suit when going out with their girlfriend.	
6.	...wears grey trousers when it's cold.	
7.	...wears a brown uniform at school.	
8.	...never wears a green jacket.	
9.	...wears a yellow belt at the disco.	
10.	...wears a black jumper when going out with their parents.	
11.	...always wears a red cap.	
12.	...wears blue sports shoes in the gym.	
13.	...wears a white swimsuit at the beach.	

UNIT 4 – ORAL PING-PONG – Person A

ENGLISH	FRENCH	ENGLISH	FRENCH
When it's cold, I wear a yellow coat.	Quand il fait froid, je porte un manteau jaune.	When it's cold, I wear a pink scarf.	Quand il fait froid, je porte une écharpe rose.
At the beach, I wear a white swimsuit.		I always wear a red swimsuit.	
When I go out with my boyfriend, I wear an orange hat.	Quand je sors avec mon petit ami, je porte un chapeau orange.	When it's hot, I wear a green hat.	Quand il fait chaud, je porte un chapeau vert.
At the gym, I wear a green t-shirt.		At the gym, I wear orange shorts.	
When I go out with my girlfriend, I wear a black tank top.	Quand je sors avec ma petite amie, je porte un tee-shirt sans manches noir.	At school, I wear a grey uniform.	Au collège, je porte un uniforme gris.
At home, I wear a blue shirt.		At the beach, I wear a black t-shirt.	
I never wear white jeans.	Je ne porte jamais de jean blanc.	When it's hot, I wear a yellow skirt.	Quand il fait chaud, je porte une jupe jaune.
When I go out with my friends, I wear green shorts.		At home, I wear red slippers.	
At the nightclub, I wear grey socks.	En discothèque, je porte des chaussettes grises.	At the nightclub, I wear an orange skirt.	En discothèque, je porte une jupe orange.
I always wear brown boots.		I always wear grey jeans.	

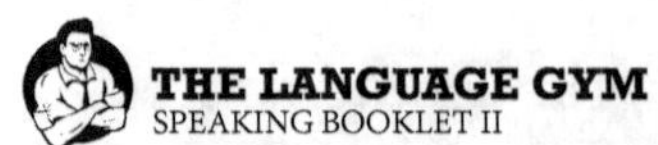

UNIT 4 – ORAL PING-PONG – Person B

ENGLISH	FRENCH	ENGLISH	FRENCH
When it's cold, I wear a yellow coat.		When it's cold, I wear a pink scarf.	
At the beach, I wear a white swimsuit.	À la plage, je porte un maillot de bain blanc.	I always wear a red swimsuit.	Je porte toujours un maillot de bain rouge.
When I go out with my boyfriend, I wear an orange hat.		When it's hot, I wear a green hat.	
At the gym, I wear a green t-shirt.	Au gymnase, je porte un tee-shirt vert.	At the gym, I wear orange shorts.	Au gymnase, je porte un short orange.
When I go out with my girlfriend, I wear a black tank top.		At school, I wear a grey uniform.	
At home, I wear a blue shirt.	À la maison, je porte une chemise bleue.	At the beach, I wear a black t-shirt.	À la plage, je porte un tee-shirt noir.
I never wear white jeans.		When it's hot, I wear a yellow skirt.	
When I go out with my friends, I wear green shorts.	Quand je sors avec mes amis, je porte un short vert.	At home, I wear red slippers.	À la maison, je porte des pantoufles rouges.
At the nightclub, I wear grey socks.		At the nightclub, I wear an orange skirt.	
I always wear brown boots.	Je porte toujours des bottes marron.	I always wear grey jeans.	Je porte toujours un jean gris.

No Snakes No Ladders

7 — When I go out with my girlfriend, I wear a white waistcoat.	8 — In school, she wears a blue skirt.	23 — I always wear a brown waistcoat.	24 — When I play football, I wear black sports shoes.
6 — When I play football, I wear black shorts.	9 — Usually, he wears a yellow necklace.	22 — When it's cold, I wear a grey coat.	25 — She never wears red boots.
5 — At school, I wear a red suit.	10 — I always wear a green watch.	21 — What clothes do you wear at home?	26 — What do you wear when you go out with your friends?
4 — I never wear a black uniform.	11 — When I play football, I wear yellow socks.	20 — When I play football, I wear orange socks.	27 — What do you wear when it's cold?
3 — When it's hot, he wears a blue baseball cap.	12 — In the gym, he wears a red t-shirt.	19 — At the nightclub, I wear red trousers.	28 — When it's hot, she wears a white swimsuit.
2 — When I go out with my friends, I wear a brown dress.	13 — I always wear a red tie.	18 — In school, I wear white earrings.	29 — When I play football, I wear a green t-shirt.
1 — In the nightclub, she wears an orange necklace.	14 — When I go out with my parents, I wear brown shorts.	17 — Usually, I wear yellow socks.	30 — What do you wear when it's hot?
START	15 — When I go out with my friends, I wear orange sports shoes.	16 — I always wear green trousers.	FINISH

No Snakes No Ladders

DÉPART

1. En discothèque, elle porte un collier orange.
2. Quand je sors avec mes amis, je porte une robe marron.
3. Quand il fait chaud, il porte une casquette bleue.
4. Je ne porte jamais d'uniforme noir.
5. Au collège, je porte un costume rouge.
6. Quand je joue au foot, je porte un short noir.
7. Quand je sors avec ma petite amie, je porte un gilet blanc.
8. Au collège, elle porte une jupe bleue.
9. D'habitude, il porte un collier jaune.
10. Je porte toujours une montre verte.
11. Quand je joue au foot, je porte des chaussettes jaunes.
12. Au gymnase, il porte un tee-shirt rouge.
13. Je porte toujours une cravate rouge.
14. Quand je sors avec mes parents, je porte un short marron.
15. Quand je sors avec mes amis, je porte des chaussures de sport orange.
16. Je porte toujours un pantalon vert.
17. D'habitude, je porte des chaussettes jaunes.
18. Au collège, je porte des boucles d'oreilles blanches.
19. En discothèque, je porte un pantalon rouge.
20. Quand je joue au foot, je porte des chaussettes orange.
21. Quels vêtements portes-tu à la maison?
22. Quand il fait froid, je porte un manteau gris.
23. Je porte toujours un gilet marron.
24. Quand je joue au foot, je porte des chaussures de sport noires.
25. Elle ne porte jamais de bottes rouges.
26. Que portes-tu quand tu sors avec amis?
27. Que portes-tu quand il fait froid?
28. Quand il fait chaud, elle porte un maillot de bain blanc.
29. Quand je joue au foot, je porte un tee-shirt vert.
30. Que portes-tu quand il fait chaud?

ARRIVÉE

UNIT 4 – STAIRCASE TRANSLATION

I always wear a blue coat and black trousers.

I always wear a blue coat and black trousers. When it's hot, I wear a white t-shirt...

I always wear a blue coat and black trousers. When it's hot, I wear a white t-shirt, red shorts and...

I always wear a blue coat and black trousers. When it's hot, I wear a white t-shirt, red shorts and a green hat. When I go out with my friends, I wear grey jeans...

I always wear a blue coat and black trousers. When it's hot, I wear a white t-shirt, red shorts and a green hat. When I go out with my friends, I wear grey jeans and a yellow shirt.

I always wear a blue coat and black trousers. When it's hot, I wear a white t-shirt, red shorts and a green hat. When I go out with my friends, I wear grey jeans and a yellow shirt. What do you wear when you go out with your friends?

Translate the last step here:

 # UNIT 4 – FASTER! 

Say:

1. I always wear a black watch.

2. I never wear a blue t-shirt.

3. When I go out with my friends, I wear black jeans.

4. Usually, I wear a yellow dress.

5. At the gym, I wear a white tracksuit.

6. At home, I wear orange slippers.

7. When I go out with my parents, I wear a grey suit.

8. When I play football, I wear black socks.

9. At the nightclub, she wears a red jacket.

10. What clothes do you wear at home?

	Time	Mistakes	Referee's name
1			
2			
3			
4			

UNIT 4 – THINGS IN COMMON

Write your own answers to the questions then interview four friends and make a note of what things you have in common.

	Moi *(Your own answer)*	1	2	3	4
Que portes-tu quand il fait chaud?					
Que portes-tu quand tu sors avec tes amis?					
Quels vêtements portes-tu à la maison?					
Que portes-tu en discothèque?					
Que portes-tu au gymnase?					
Que portes-tu à la plage?					
Que portes-tu quand tu sors avec tes parents?					
Que portes-tu quand il fait froid?					
Tu portes une cravate au collège?					

UNIT 4 – COMMUNICATIVE DRILLS

1	2	3
What do you wear when it's cold? - When it's cold, I wear a red jumper. **What clothes do you wear when you go out with friends?** - I always wear a blue tracksuit.	**What clothes do you wear at home?** - At home, I wear a white t-shirt and blue jeans. **What clothes do you wear at the gym?** - Usually, I wear a white t-shirt and grey shorts.	**What do you wear when it's hot?** - Usually, I wear a yellow swimsuit. **Describe your school uniform.** - At school, I wear a grey suit and a green tie.

4	5	6
What do you wear when you go out with your boyfriend? - I wear a black skirt and a grey shirt. What clothes do you wear when you go out with your girlfriend? **When I go out with my girlfriend, I wear a blue suit.**	**Describe your school uniform.** - In school, I wear a brown jacket and blue trousers. **Do you wear a tie?** - Yes, I wear an orange tie and black shoes.	**When I go out with my friends I wear a yellow sports jacket. And you?** - I never wear a sports jacket. I always wear a red jumper with red high heel shoes.

7	8	9
What do you wear when you play football? - I always wear blue socks and a black tracksuit. And you? **When I play football, I wear an orange tank top and green sports shoes.**	**What do you wear when you go out with your parents?** - I usually wear a white cap. **What do you wear when it's cold?** - When it's cold, I wear a red coat.	**What do you wear at the beach?** - At the beach, I wear a black swimsuit and a green hat. And you? **Usually, I wear a red cap and brown sandals.**

UNIT 4 – COMMUNICATIVE DRILLS REFEREE CARD

1	2	3
Que portes-tu quand il fait froid? - Quand il fait froid, je porte un pull rouge. **Que portes-tu quand tu sors avec tes amis?** - Je porte toujours un survêtement bleu.	**Quels vêtements portes-tu à la maison?** - À la maison, je porte un tee-shirt blanc et un jean bleu. **Que portes-tu au gymnase?** - D'habitude je porte un tee-shirt blanc et un short gris.	**Que portes-tu quand il fait chaud?** - D'habitude, je porte un maillot de bain jaune. **Décris ton uniforme scolaire.** - Au collège, je porte un costume gris et une cravate verte.
4	**5**	**6**
Que portes-tu quand tu sors avec ton petit ami? - Je porte une jupe noire et une chemise grise. Que portes-tu quand tu sors avec ta petite amie? **Quand je sors avec ma petite amie, je porte un costume bleu.**	**Décris ton uniforme scolaire.** - Au collège, je porte une veste marron et un pantalon bleu. **Tu portes une cravate?** - Oui, je porte une cravate orange et des chaussures noires.	**Quand je sors avec mes amis, je porte une veste de sport jaune. Et toi?** - Je ne porte jamais de veste de sport. Je porte toujours un pull rouge avec des chaussures à talons hauts rouges.
7	**8**	**9**
Que portes-tu quand tu joues au foot? - Je porte toujours des chaussettes bleues et un survêtement noir. Et toi? **Quand je joue au foot, je porte un tee-shirt sans manches orange et des chaussures de sport vertes.**	**Que portes-tu quand tu sors avec tes parents?** - D'habitude, je porte une casquette blanche. **Que portes-tu quand il fait froid?** - Quand il fait froid, je porte un manteau rouge.	**Que portes-tu à la plage?** - À la plage, je porte un maillot de bain noir et un chapeau vert. Et toi? **D'habitude, je porte une casquette rouge et des sandales marron.**

UNIT 4 – SURVEY

	Comment tu t'appelles? *What is your name?*	Que portes-tu quand il fait chaud? *What do you wear when it's hot?*	Quels vêtements portes-tu à la maison? *What clothes do you wear at home?*	Que portes-tu quand tu joues au foot? *What do you wear when you play football?*	Que portes-tu au gymnase? *What do you wear at the gym?*	Que portes-tu quand tu sors avec tes amis? *What do you wear when you go out with your friends?*
e.g.	*Je m'appelle Jean.*	*Quand il fait chaud, je porte un tee-shirt blanc.*	*À la maison, je porte un survêtement gris.*	*Je porte toujours un short blanc et un tee-shirt bleu.*	*Au gymnase, je porte un tee-shirt sans manches orange.*	*Quand je sors avec mes amis, je porte une veste noire.*
1.						
2.						
3.						
4.						
5.						
6.						
7.						

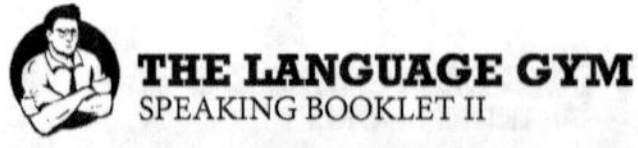

UNIT 4 – ANSWERS

FIND SOMEONE WHO

Find someone who…		Name(s)
1.	…wears a red scarf when it's cold.	**Charles/Aurore**
2.	…wears a white t-shirt when it's hot.	**Anthony**
3.	…wears orange shorts at home.	**Jean/Alice**
4.	…wears white shorts when playing football.	**Martine**
5.	…wears a blue suit when going out with their girlfriend.	**Michel**
6.	…wears grey trousers when it's cold.	**Hélène**
7.	…wears a brown uniform at school.	**Léa**
8.	…never wears a green jacket.	**Georges**
9.	…wears a yellow belt at the disco.	**Joël**
10.	…wears a black jumper when going out with their parents.	**Laure**
11.	…always wears a red cap.	**Julie**
12.	…wears blue sports shoes in the gym.	**Fernand**
13.	…wears a white swimsuit at the beach.	**Lucie**

STAIRCASE TRANSLATION

Je porte toujours un manteau bleu et un pantalon noir. Quand il fait chaud, je porte un tee-shirt blanc, un short rouge et un chapeau vert. Quand je sors avec mes amis, je porte un jean gris et une chemise jaune. Que portes-tu quand tu sors avec tes amis?

FASTER!

REFEREE SOLUTION:

1. Je porte toujours une montre noire.
2. Je ne porte jamais de tee-shirt bleu.
3. Quand je sors avec mes amis, je porte un jean noir.
4. D'habitude, je porte une robe jaune.
5. Au gymnase, je porte un survêtement blanc.
6. À la maison, je porte des pantoufles orange.
7. Quand je sors avec mes parents, je porte un costume gris.
8. Quand je joue au foot, je porte des chaussettes noires.
9. En discothèque, elle porte une veste rouge.
10. Quels vêtements portes-tu à la maison?

THINGS IN COMMON

Students give their own answers to the questions and make a note of which students they have things in common with.

UNIT 5.
My weekend plans – food & leisure

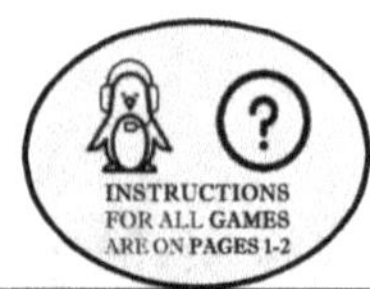

Que vas-tu faire ce week-end?	*What are you going to do this weekend?*
Tu penses que ce sera comment?	*What do you think it will be like?*
Que vas-tu prendre pour le petit-déjeuner?	*What are you going to have for breakfast?*
Que manges-tu d'habitude pour le déjeuner?	*What do you usually eat for lunch?*
Qu'est-ce que tu aimes boire?	*What do you like to drink?*

Ce week-end *This weekend* **Demain** *Tomorrow* **Samedi/dimanche prochain** *Next Saturday/Sunday*	**je vais** *I am going* **ma famille et moi allons** *my family and I are going*	**aller** *to go*	**au centre commercial** **au restaurant** **à un concert**	*to the mall* *to a restaurant* *to a concert*
		faire *to do*	**beaucoup de choses** **les magasins** **du sport**	*many things* *shopping* *sport*
		jouer *to play*	**au foot** **aux jeux vidéo** **de la guitare** **du piano**	*football* *videogames* *the guitar* *the piano*
		regarder *to watch*	**un film** **un match** **une série sur Netflix**	*a film* *a match* *a series on Netflix*

Je pense que ce sera *I think that it will be*	**assez** *quite* **très** *very*	**amusant** **divertissant** **ennuyeux** **intéressant**	*fun* *entertaining* *boring* *interesting*
Je pense que ce ne sera pas *I think that it won't be*			

Pour le petit-déjeuner *For breakfast*	**j'adore** *I love*	**manger** *to eat* **prendre** *to have*	**des céréales avec du lait** **des fruits** **du jambon** **du miel** **du poisson** **du poulet rôti** **du fromage** **un sandwich** **une salade** **un croissant** **une tartine**	*cereal with milk* *fruit* *ham* *honey* *fish* *roast chicken* *cheese* *a sandwich* *a salad* *a croissant* *a slice of bread*
Pour le déjeuner *For lunch*	**j'aime** *I like*			
Pour le dîner *For dinner*	**je vais** *I am going (to)*	**boire** *to drink* **prendre** *to have*	**de l'eau** **du café** **du chocolat chaud** **un verre de lait** **une tasse de thé** **un jus d'orange**	*water* *coffee* *hot chocolate* *a glass of milk* *a cup of tea* *an orange juice*

UNIT 5 – FIND SOMEONE WHO – Student Cards

Ce week-end, je vais aller au restaurant. **ARTHUR**	Samedi prochain, je vais faire du sport. **PHILIPPE**	Dimanche, ma famille et moi allons aller à un concert. **JEANNE**	Je vais aller au centre commercial avec ma famille dimanche prochain. **BÉATRICE**
Pour le dîner, je vais prendre du poulet rôti. **FRANCIS**	Samedi, je vais faire beaucoup de choses. **JULES**	Dimanche prochain, je vais faire les magasins. **CATHERINE**	Pour le déjeuner, j'aime manger un sandwich. **ANNA**
Pour le dîner, je vais manger du poisson. **FRANÇOIS**	Ce week-end, je vais regarder une série sur Netflix. **SOPHIE**	Ce week-end, je vais jouer de la guitare. **ÉMILIE**	Dimanche, je vais aller à un concert. **OLIVIA**
Dimanche prochain, ma famille et moi allons aller au centre commercial. **GUILLAUME**	Pour le petit-déjeuner, je vais boire du café. **LOUIS**	Samedi, je vais faire beaucoup de choses. **MARION**	Dimanche prochain, je vais jouer aux jeux vidéo. **CARMEN**

UNIT 5 – FIND SOMEONE WHO – Student Grid

Que vas-tu faire ce week-end?	*What are you going to do this weekend?*
Que vas-tu prendre pour le petit-déjeuner?	*What are you going to have for breakfast?*
Que manges-tu d'habitude pour le déjeuner?	*What do you usually eat for lunch?*

Find someone who...		Name(s)
1.	...is going to play videogames next Sunday.	
2.	...likes to eat a sandwich for lunch.	
3.	...is going to go to a concert on Sunday.	
4.	...is going to have roast chicken for dinner.	
5.	...is going to go shopping next Sunday.	
6.	...is going to do many things on Saturday.	
7.	...is going to watch a series on Netflix this weekend.	
8.	...is going to drink coffee for breakfast.	
9.	...is going to play the guitar this weekend.	
10.	...is going to go to a restaurant this weekend.	
11.	...is going to do sport next Saturday.	
12.	...is going to eat fish for dinner.	
13.	...is going to the mall with their family next Sunday.	

UNIT 5 – ORAL PING-PONG – Person A

ENGLISH	FRENCH	ENGLISH	FRENCH
This weekend, I am going to go to the mall.	Ce week-end, je vais aller au centre commercial.	For breakfast, I am going to drink a glass of milk.	Pour le petit-déjeuner, je vais boire un verre de lait.
Next Saturday, we are going to do sport.		For dinner, I like to eat roast chicken.	
On Saturday, I am going to play the guitar.	Samedi, je vais jouer de la guitare.	For lunch, I like to drink water.	Pour le déjeuner, j'aime boire de l'eau.
On Sunday, we are going to watch a football match.		For breakfast, I love to eat fruit.	
This weekend, we are going to do many things.	Ce week-end, nous allons faire beaucoup de choses.	This weekend, I am going to watch a series on Netflix.	Ce week-end, je vais regarder une série sur Netflix.
I think it will be very fun.		For lunch, I like to drink water.	
For dinner, I am going to have fish.	Pour le dîner, je vais prendre du poisson.	On Sunday, we are going to go to the restaurant.	Dimanche, nous allons aller au restaurant.
Next Saturday, I am going to play videogames.		For breakfast, I am going to have hot chocolate.	
On Saturday, I am going to do homework.	Samedi, je vais faire mes devoirs.	I think it won't be interesting.	Je pense que ce ne sera pas intéressant.
For lunch, I like to eat a salad.		For breakfast, I am going to drink tea.	

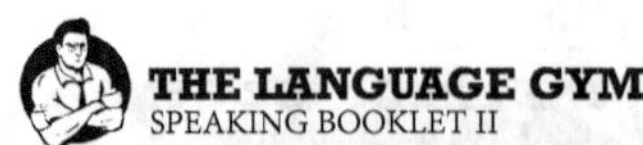

UNIT 5 – ORAL PING-PONG – Person B

ENGLISH	FRENCH	ENGLISH	FRENCH
This weekend, I am going to go to the mall.		**For breakfast, I am going to drink a glass of milk.**	
Next Saturday, we are going to do sport.	Samedi prochain, nous allons faire du sport.	**For dinner, I like to eat roast chicken.**	Pour le dîner, j'aime manger du poulet rôti.
On Saturday, I am going to play the guitar.		**For lunch, I like to drink water.**	
On Sunday, we are going to watch a football match.	Dimanche, nous allons regarder un match de foot.	**For breakfast, I love to eat fruit.**	Pour le petit-déjeuner, j'adore manger des fruits.
This weekend, we are going to do many things.		**This weekend, I am going to watch a series on Netflix.**	
I think it will be very fun.	Je pense que ce sera très amusant.	**For lunch, I like to drink water.**	Pour le déjeuner, j'aime boire de l'eau.
For dinner, I am going to have fish.		**On Sunday, we are going to go to the restaurant.**	
Next Saturday, I am going to play videogames.	Samedi prochain, je vais jouer aux jeux vidéo.	**For breakfast, I am going to have hot chocolate.**	Pour le petit-déjeuner, je vais prendre du chocolat chaud.
On Saturday, I am going to do homework.		**I think it won't be interesting.**	
For lunch, I like to eat a salad.	Pour le déjeuner, j'aime manger une salade.	**For breakfast, I am going to drink tea.**	Pour le petit-déjeuner, je vais boire du thé.

No Snakes No Ladders

1 — For lunch, I like to eat a salad.

2 — For lunch, I like to drink water.

3 — For breakfast, I am going to have hot chocolate.

4 — For breakfast, I am going to drink tea.

5 — For dinner, I love to eat roast chicken.

6 — For breakfast, I like to eat fruit.

7 — I think it will be very fun.

8 — What are you going to do this weekend?

9 — For lunch, I like to eat cheese.

10 — For dinner, I am going to have fish.

11 — On Saturday, I am going to do my homework.

12 — This weekend, we are going to do many things.

13 — This weekend, I am going to watch a series on Netflix.

14 — Next Saturday, we are going to do sport.

15 — This weekend, we are going to go to the mall.

START

16 — Next Saturday, I am going to play videogames.

17 — On Sunday, we are going to go to the restaurant.

18 — On Saturday, I am going to play the guitar.

19 — What are you going to have for breakfast?

20 — For lunch, I like to eat a sandwich.

21 — On Sunday, we are going to watch a football match.

22 — How do you think it will be?

23 — For breakfast, I am going to drink a glass of milk.

24 — For breakfast, I am going to have coffee.

25 — On Saturday, we are going to go shopping at the mall.

26 — On Sunday we are going to go to a concert.

27 — For dinner, I am going to eat fish.

28 — What do you usually eat for lunch?

29 — What do you like to drink?

30 — On Saturday we are going to play the piano.

FINISH

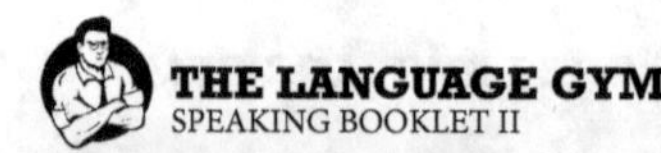

No Snakes No Ladders

DÉPART

1 — Pour le déjeuner, j'aime manger une salade.

2 — Pour le déjeuner, j'aime boire de l'eau.

3 — Pour le petit-déjeuner, je vais prendre du chocolat chaud.

4 — Pour le petit-déjeuner, je vais boire du thé.

5 — Pour le dîner, j'adore manger du poulet rôti.

6 — Pour le petit-déjeuner, j'aime manger des fruits.

7 — Je pense que ce sera très amusant.

8 — Que vas-tu faire ce week-end?

9 — Pour le déjeuner, j'aime manger du fromage.

10 — Pour le dîner, je vais prendre du poisson.

11 — Samedi, je vais faire mes devoirs.

12 — Ce week-end, nous allons faire beaucoup de choses.

13 — Ce week-end, je vais regarder une série sur Netflix.

14 — Samedi prochain, nous allons faire du sport.

15 — Ce week-end, nous allons aller au centre commercial.

16 — Samedi prochain, je vais jouer aux jeux vidéo.

17 — Dimanche, nous allons aller au restaurant.

18 — Samedi, je vais jouer de la guitare.

19 — Que vas-tu prendre pour le petit-déjeuner?

20 — Pour le déjeuner, j'aime manger un sandwich.

21 — Dimanche, nous allons regarder un match de foot.

22 — Tu penses que ce sera comment?

23 — Pour le petit-déjeuner, je vais boire un verre de lait.

24 — Pour le petit-déjeuner, je vais prendre du café.

25 — Samedi, nous allons faire les magasins au centre commercial.

26 — Dimanche, nous allons aller à un concert.

27 — Pour le dîner, je vais manger du poisson.

28 — Que manges-tu d'habitude pour le déjeuner?

29 — Qu'est-ce que tu aimes boire?

30 — Samedi, nous allons jouer du piano.

ARRIVÉE

UNIT 5 – STAIRCASE TRANSLATION

This weekend...

This weekend, I'm going to go to a restaurant.

This weekend, I'm going to go to a restaurant. I think it will be very fun.

This weekend, I'm going to go to a restaurant. I think it will be very fun. For dinner, I like to eat...

This weekend, I'm going to go to a restaurant. I think it will be very fun. For dinner, I like to eat roast chicken and a salad.

This weekend, I'm going to go to a restaurant. I think it will be very fun. For dinner, I like to eat roast chicken and a salad. Next Sunday, my family and I are going to go shopping.

Translate the last step here:

 UNIT 5 – FASTER! 

Say:

1. What are you going to do this weekend?

2. This weekend, I'm going to go shopping.

3. On Saturday, I'm going to play videogames.

4. What do you like to drink?

5. For breakfast, I like to drink coffee.

6. For lunch, I like to eat a sandwich.

7. I think it will be quite fun.

8. Next Sunday, my family and I are going to go to a concert.

	Time	Mistakes	Referee's name
1			
2			
3			
4			

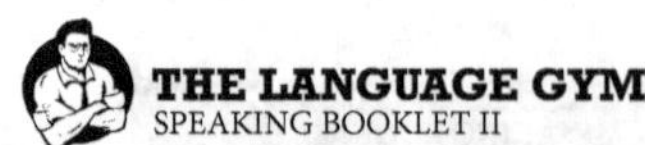

UNIT 5 – FAST & FURIOUS

(Fill in the missing verbs)

ROUND 1

1. Samedi, nous allons __________ au centre commercial.
2. Ce week-end, je vais __________ du sport.
3. Dimanche prochain, nous allons ______________ un match de foot.
4. Ce week-end, je vais __________ de la guitare.
5. Samedi, ma famille et moi allons ____________ au restaurant.
6. Dimanche, nous allons ____________ une série sur Netflix.
7. Je vais __________ mes devoirs samedi.
8. Samedi, je vais ____________ au foot.
9. Dimanche prochain, ma famille et moi allons __________ les magasins.
10. Ce week-end, nous allons __________ à un concert.

	Time 1	Time 2	Time 3	Time 4
Time				
Mistakes				

ROUND 2

1. Ce week-end, je vais ____________ les magasins.
2. Samedi prochain, nous allons ____________ au foot.
3. Samedi, nous allons ____________ un match de foot.
4. Ce week-end, ma famille et moi allons ____________ beaucoup de choses.
5. Dimanche, je vais ______________ de la guitare.
6. Ce week-end, je vais ______________ une série sur Netflix.
7. Samedi, je vais__________ aux jeux vidéo.
8. Ma famille et moi allons ______________ à un concert.
9. Ce week-end, nous allons ______________ un film.
10. Demain, pour le déjeuner, je vais __________ un sandwich et __________ de l'eau.

	Time 1	Time 2	Time 3	Time 4
Time				
Mistakes				

UNIT 5 – COMMUNICATIVE DRILLS

1	2	3
What are you going to do this weekend? - This weekend, I'm going to play the guitar. **What do you think it will be like?** - I think it will be very fun.	**What do you usually have for breakfast?** - For breakfast, I like to eat fruit. And you? **I usually like to eat cereal with milk. For dinner, I love to eat roast chicken!**	**What do you usually eat for lunch?** - For lunch, I usually eat a sandwich and a salad. **What do you like to drink?** -I like to drink tea or coffee.

4	5	6
What do you like to eat for dinner? - For dinner, I like to eat fish or ham. **What do you like to drink?** - For dinner, I like to drink water.	**What are you going to do this weekend?** - On Saturday, I'm going to go shopping. **And Sunday?** - On Sunday, my family and I are going to play videogames.	**What are you going to do on Sunday?** - On Sunday, I'm going to go to a concert. And you? **My family and I are going to play football.**

7	8	9
What are you going to eat for dinner? - For dinner, I am going to eat roast chicken and a salad. **What are you going to drink?** - I am going to drink an orange juice.	**What are you going to do next Saturday?** - Next Saturday, I'm going to do many things. And you? **I'm going to do sport. I think it will be very fun!**	**What do you usually have for lunch?** - For lunch, I usually eat cheese and ham. This weekend, I'm going to eat a croissant. **I like croissants. I'm also going to eat fruit and honey.**

UNIT 5 – COMMUNICATIVE DRILLS
REFEREE CARD

1	2	3
Que vas-tu faire ce week-end? - Ce week-end, je vais jouer de la guitare. **Tu penses que ce sera comment?** - Je pense que ce sera très amusant.	**Que manges-tu d'habitude pour le petit-déjeuner?** - Pour le petit-déjeuner, j'aime manger des fruits. Et toi? **D'habitude, j'aime manger des céréales avec du lait. Pour le dîner, j'adore manger du poulet rôti!**	**Que manges-tu d'habitude pour le déjeuner?** - Pour le déjeuner, d'habitude, je mange un sandwich et une salade. **Qu'est-ce que tu aimes boire?** - J'aime boire du thé ou du café.
4	**5**	**6**
Qu'est-ce que tu aimes manger pour le dîner? -Pour le dîner, j'aime manger du poisson ou du jambon. **Qu'est-ce que tu aimes boire?** - Pour le dîner, j'aime boire de l'eau.	**Que vas-tu faire ce week-end?** - Samedi, je vais faire les magasins. **Et dimanche?** - Dimanche, ma famille et moi allons jouer aux jeux vidéo.	**Que vas-tu faire dimanche?** - Dimanche, je vais aller à un concert. Et toi? **Ma famille et moi allons jouer au foot.**
7	**8**	**9**
Que vas-tu manger pour le dîner? - Pour le dîner, je vais manger du poulet rôti et une salade. **Que vas-tu boire?** Je vais boire un jus d'orange.	**Que vas-tu faire samedi prochain?** - Samedi prochain, je vais faire beaucoup de choses. Et toi? **Je vais faire du sport. Je pense que ce sera très amusant!**	**Que manges-tu d'habitude pour le déjeuner?** - Pour le déjeuner, d'habitude, je mange du fromage et du jambon. Ce week-end, je vais manger un croissant. **J'aime les croissants. Je vais aussi manger des fruits et du miel.**

UNIT 5 – SURVEY

	Comment tu t'appelles? *What is your name?*	Que vas-tu faire ce week-end? *What are you going to do this weekend?*	Que manges-tu d'habitude pour le petit-déjeuner? *What do you usually eat for breakfast?*	Qu'est-ce que tu aimes boire? *What do you like to drink?*	Que manges-tu d'habitude pour le déjeuner? *What do you usually eat for lunch?*	Que vas-tu manger pour le dîner? *What are you going to eat for dinner?*
e.g.	*Je m'appelle Jean.*	*Ce week-end, je vais aller au restaurant.*	*Pour le petit-déjeuner, d'habitude, je mange une tartine avec du miel.*	*J'aime boire du café.*	*Pour le déjeuner, d'habitude, j'aime manger une salade.*	*Pour le dîner, je vais manger du poisson.*
1.						
2.						
3.						
4.						
5.						
6.						
7.						

UNIT 5 – ANSWERS

FIND SOMEONE WHO

	Find someone who...	Name(s)
1.	...is going to play videogames next Sunday.	**Carmen**
2.	...likes to eat a sandwich for lunch.	**Anna**
3.	...is going to go to a concert on Sunday.	**Jeanne/Olivia**
4.	...is going to have roast chicken for dinner.	**Francis**
5.	...is going to go shopping next Sunday.	**Catherine**
6.	...is going to do many things this Saturday.	**Jules/Marion**
7.	...is going to watch a series on Netflix this weekend.	**Sophie**
8.	...is going to drink coffee for breakfast.	**Louis**
9.	...is going to play the guitar this weekend.	**Émilie**
10.	...is going to go to a restaurant this weekend.	**Arthur**
11.	...is going to do sport next Saturday.	**Philippe**
12.	...is going to eat fish for dinner.	**François**
13.	...is going to the mall with their family next Sunday.	**Béatrice/Guillaume**

STAIRCASE TRANSLATION

Ce week-end, je vais aller au restaurant. Je pense que ce sera très amusant. Pour le dîner, j'aime manger du poulet rôti et une salade. Dimanche prochain, ma famille et moi allons faire les magasins.

FASTER! REFEREE SOLUTION:

1. Que vas-tu faire ce week-end?   2. Ce week-end, je vais faire les magasins.
3. Samedi, je vais jouer aux jeux vidéo.   4. Qu'est-ce que tu aimes boire?
5. Pour le petit-déjeuner, j'aime boire du café.   6. Pour le déjeuner, j'aime manger un sandwich.
7. Je pense que ce sera assez amusant.   8. Dimanche prochain, ma famille et moi allons aller à un concert.

FAST & FURIOUS

ROUND 1

1. Samedi, nous allons **aller** au centre commercial.   2. Ce week-end, je vais **faire** du sport
3. Dimanche prochain, nous allons **regarder** un match de foot.   4. Ce week-end, je vais **jouer** de la guitare.
5. Samedi, ma famille et moi allons **aller/manger** au restaurant.
6. Dimanche, nous allons **regarder** une série sur Netflix.   7. Je vais **faire** mes devoirs samedi.
8. Samedi, je vais **jouer** au foot.   9. Dimanche prochain, ma famille et moi allons **faire** les magasins.
10. Ce week-end, nous allons **aller** à un concert.

ROUND 2

1. Ce week-end, je vais **faire** les magasins.   2. Samedi prochain, nous allons **jouer** au foot.
3. Samedi, nous allons **regarder** un match de foot.
4. Ce week-end, ma famille et moi allons **faire** beaucoup de choses.   5. Dimanche, je vais **jouer** de la guitare.
6. Ce week-end, je vais **regarder** une série sur Netflix.   7. Samedi, je vais **jouer** aux jeux vidéo.
8. Ma famille et moi allons **aller** à un concert.   9. Ce week-end, nous allons **regarder** un film.
10. Demain, pour le déjeuner, je vais **manger** un sandwich et **boire** de l'eau.

UNIT 6.
Saying where I live

Où habites-tu?	Where do you live?
Qu'est-ce qu'il y a dans ta ville?	What is there in your city?
Tu aimes ton quartier? Pourquoi?	Do you like your neighbourhood? Why?

| J'habite à
I live in

Nous habitons à
We live in | Berlin
Dublin
Édimbourg
Londres
Madrid
Nice
Paris
Rome | C'est dans
It is in | le centre
le nord
l'est
le sud
l'ouest
le nord-ouest
le sud-est | de l'Allemagne
de l'Australie
de l'Écosse
de l'Espagne
de la France
du Pays de Galles
de l'Angleterre
de l'Irlande
de l'Italie |

Près de chez moi *Near my house* Dans ma ville *In my city* Dans le centre *In the centre* Dans mon quartier *In my neighbourhood* Dans ma rue *On my street*	il y a *there is/are* il n'y a pas (de) *there isn't/ aren't*	un aquarium *an aquarium* beaucoup de jeunes *lots of young people* des cafés *cafés* un centre commercial *a mall* des restaurants *restaurants* une rue piétonne *a pedestrian street*	un centre sportif *a sports centre* un cinéma *a cinema* un club de jeunes *a youth club* un grand parc *a big park* un jardin botanique *a botanical garden*
		beaucoup à faire pour les jeunes *a lot to do for young people* beaucoup de choses à faire *many things to do* beaucoup de choses à voir *many things to see*	
	nous avons *we have* nous n'avons pas *we do not have*	beaucoup de/d' plein de/d' *a lot of/many*	jolies rues — *pretty streets* installations sportives *sports facilities* magasins — *shops* restaurants — *restaurants* vieux bâtiments — *old buildings*

J'aime mon quartier car *I like my neighbourhood because* Je n'aime pas mon quartier car *I don't like my neighbourhood because*	c'est *it is*	dangereux — *dangerous* sûr — *safe*
	il est *it is*	bien tenu — *well kept* mal tenu — *badly kept* propre — *clean* sale — *dirty*
	il (n') y a (pas) *there is -not-*	beaucoup de bruit — *a lot of noise* beaucoup de circulation — *a lot of traffic* beaucoup de pollution — *a lot of pollution*
	on (ne) peut (pas) *one can -not-*	bien manger — *eat well* faire du sport — *do sport* se promener — *go for a walk*

UNIT 6 – FIND SOMEONE WHO – Student Cards

Dans le centre, il y a un centre sportif. **PIERRE**	Dans ma rue, il y a un club de jeunes. **ALEXANDRE**	Dans ma ville, nous n'avons pas d'aquarium. **MARTINE**	Dans le centre de ma ville, il y a une rue piétonne. **PATRICIA**
Près de chez moi, il y a un cinéma moderne. **ROSANNE**	Il y a beaucoup de choses à faire dans mon quartier. **PAUL**	Dans mon quartier, nous avons un centre sportif. **JEAN**	Dans ma rue, il y a beaucoup de restaurants. **MICHEL**
Dans mon quartier, il y a beaucoup de choses à faire. **CARLA**	Près de chez moi, il y a un parc. **RAPHAËL**	Dans le centre de ma ville, il y a un centre sportif. **XAVIER**	Près de chez moi, il y a un cinéma. **ANDRÉA**
Il n'y a pas d'aquarium dans ma ville. **PERRINE**	Dans ma ville, nous avons un centre commercial. **VALÉRIE**	Dans ma ville, il y a un jardin botanique. **BRUNO**	Dans mon quartier, nous avons beaucoup de vieux bâtiments. **LIONEL**

UNIT 6 – FIND SOMEONE WHO – Student Grid

Où habites-tu? Qu'est-ce qu'il y a dans ta ville?	*Where do you live?* *What is there in your city?*	
Find someone who...		**Name(s)**
1.	...has a pedestrian street in their city centre.	
2.	...has a shopping centre in their city.	
3.	...has lots of old buildings in their neighbourhood.	
4.	...has many things to do in their neighbourhood.	
5.	...has lots of restaurants on their street.	
6.	...has a sports centre in the city centre.	
7.	...has a youth club on their street.	
8.	...doesn't have an aquarium in their city.	
9.	...lives near a park.	
10.	...lives near a cinema.	
11.	...has a sports centre in their neighbourhood.	
12.	...has a botanical garden in their city.	

UNIT 6 – ORAL PING-PONG – Person A

ENGLISH	FRENCH	ENGLISH	FRENCH
I live in Berlin. It's in the east of Germany.	J'habite à Berlin. C'est dans l'est de l'Allemagne.	I like my neighbourhood because one can do sport.	J'aime mon quartier parce qu'on peut faire du sport.
We live in Cardiff. It's in the south of Wales.		I don't like my neighbourhood because there is a lot of pollution.	
In my city, there are many things to do.	Dans ma ville, il y a beaucoup de choses à faire.	I live in Rome, it's in the west of Italy.	J'habite à Rome, c'est dans l'ouest de l'Italie.
In the centre of my neighbourhood, there is a pedestrian street.		In my city, we don't have an aquarium.	
On my street, there aren't many young people.	Dans ma rue, il n'y a pas beaucoup de jeunes.	In my city, we have many restaurants.	Dans ma ville, nous avons beaucoup de restaurants.
I don't like my neighbourhood because it's dangerous.		I live in Paris. It's in the north of France.	
I like my neighbourhood because it's clean.	J'aime mon quartier parce que c'est propre.	Near my house, there is a park.	Près de chez moi, il y a un parc.
I don't like my neighbourhood because there is a lot of noise.		I like my neighbourhood because one can go for a walk.	
I live in Madrid. It's in the centre of Spain.	J'habite à Madrid. C'est dans le centre de l'Espagne.	In my city, we have a cinema.	Dans ma ville, nous avons un cinéma.
We live in Edinburgh. It's in the south of Scotland.		I live in London. It's in the southeast of England.	

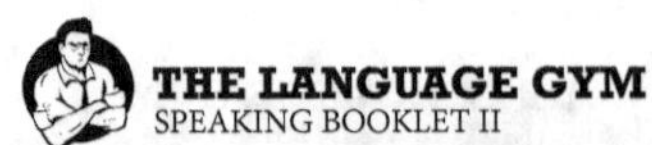

UNIT 6 – ORAL PING-PONG – Person B

ENGLISH	FRENCH	ENGLISH	FRENCH
I live in Berlin. It's in the east of Germany.		I like my neighbourhood because one can do sport.	
We live in Cardiff. It's in the south of Wales.	Nous habitons à Cardiff. C'est dans le sud du Pays de Galles.	I don't like my neighbourhood because there is a lot of pollution.	Je n'aime pas mon quartier parce qu'il y a beaucoup de pollution.
In my city, there are many things to do.		I live in Rome, it's in the west of Italy.	
In the centre of my neighbourhood, there is a pedestrian street.	Dans le centre de mon quartier, il y a une rue piétonne.	In my city, we don't have an aquarium.	Dans ma ville, nous n'avons pas d'aquarium.
On my street, there aren't many young people.		In my city, we have many restaurants.	
I don't like my neighbourhood because it's dangerous.	Je n'aime pas mon quartier parce que c'est dangereux.	I live in Paris. It's in the north of France.	J'habite à Paris. C'est dans le nord de la France.
I like my neighbourhood because it's clean.		Near my house, there is a park.	
I don't like my neighbourhood because there is a lot of noise.	Je n'aime pas mon quartier parce qu'il y a beaucoup de bruit.	I like my neighbourhood because one can go for a walk.	J'aime mon quartier car on peut se promener.
I live in Madrid. It's in the centre of Spain.		In my city, we have a cinema.	
We live in Edinburgh. It's in the south of Scotland.	Nous habitons à Édimbourg. C'est dans le sud de l'Écosse.	I live in London. It's in the southeast of England.	J'habite à Londres. C'est dans le sud-est de l'Angleterre.

No Snakes No Ladders

START

1 — We live in Cardiff. It is in the south of Wales.

2 — I live in Berlin. It is in the east of Germany.

3 — In my neighbourhood there are lots of shops.

4 — In my city, there is a lot of traffic.

5 — Near my house, there is a botanical garden.

6 — Where do you live?

7 — I like my neighbourhood because there isn't much noise.

8 — I don't like my neighbourhood because it's dangerous.

9 — In my city, we don't have a shopping centre.

10 — In my city, we have many shops.

11 — What is there in your city?

12 — I don't like my neighbourhood because there is a lot of pollution.

13 — I like my neighbourhood because one can do sport.

14 — I live in Rome. It's in the west of Italy.

15 — I live in London. It's in the southeast of England.

16 — On my street, there aren't many old buildings.

17 — Is there a lot of traffic in your city?

18 — I like my neighbourhood because it's clean.

19 — I like my neighbourhood because there isn't much noise.

20 — We live in Edinburgh. It's in the south of Scotland.

21 — I live in Paris. It's in the north of France.

22 — I don't like my neighbourhood because one can't do sport.

23 — Are there old buildings?

24 — I live in London. It's very dirty.

25 — In my city, there is a lot of noise.

26 — Do you like your neighbourhood? Why?

27 — I like my neighbourhood because one can go for a walk.

28 — I live in Madrid. It's in the centre of Spain.

29 — In my city we have an aquarium.

30 — What can one do in your neighbourhood?

FINISH

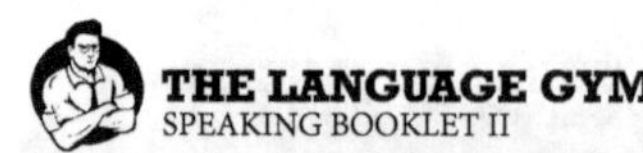

No Snakes No Ladders

DÉPART

1
Nous habitons à Cardiff. C'est dans le sud du Pays de Galles.

2
J'habite à Berlin. C'est dans l'est de l'Allemagne.

3
Dans mon quartier, il y a beaucoup de magasins.

4
Dans ma ville, il y a beaucoup de circulation.

5
Près de chez moi, il y a un jardin botanique.

6
Où habites-tu?

7
J'aime mon quartier car il n'y a pas beaucoup de bruit.

8
Je n'aime pas mon quartier parce que c'est dangereux.

9
Dans ma ville, nous n'avons pas de centre commercial.

10
Dans ma ville, nous avons beaucoup de magasins.

11
Qu'est-ce qu'il y a dans ta ville?

12
Je n'aime pas mon quartier parce qu'il y a beaucoup de pollution.

13
J'aime mon quartier parce qu'on peut faire du sport.

14
J'habite à Rome. C'est dans l'ouest de l'Italie.

15
J'habite à Londres. C'est dans le sud-est de l'Angleterre.

16
Dans ma rue, il n'y a pas beaucoup de vieux bâtiments.

17
Il y a beaucoup de circulation dans ta ville?

18
J'aime mon quartier parce que c'est propre.

19
J'aime mon quartier car il n'y a pas beaucoup de bruit.

20
Nous habitons à Édimbourg. C'est dans le sud de l'Écosse.

21
J'habite à Paris. C'est dans le nord de la France.

22
Je n'aime pas mon quartier car on ne peut pas faire de sport.

23
Il y a des vieux bâtiments?

24
J'habite à Londres. C'est très sale.

25
Dans ma ville, il y a beaucoup de bruit.

26
Tu aimes ton quartier? Pourquoi?

27
J'aime mon quartier car on peut se promener.

28
J'habite à Madrid, c'est dans le centre de l'Espagne.

29
Dans ma ville, nous avons un aquarium.

30
Qu'est-ce qu'on peut faire dans ton quartier?

ARRIVÉE

UNIT 6 – STAIRCASE TRANSLATION

I live in London. It is in the southeast of England.

I live in London. It is in the southeast of England. In my neighbourhood, there are many things to do.

I live in London. It is in the southeast of England. In my neighbourhood, there are many things to do. I like my neighbourhood because it is clean.

I live in London. It is in the southeast of England. In my neighbourhood, there are many things to do. I like my neighbourhood because it is clean. On my street, there is a park.

I live in London. It is in the southeast of England. In my neighbourhood, there are many things to do. I like my neighbourhood because it is clean. On my street, there is a park. In the centre there is a cinema and lots of shops.

I live in London. It is in the southeast of England. In my neighbourhood, there are many things to do. I like my neighbourhood because it is clean. On my street, there is a park. In the centre, there is a cinema and lots of shops. I like my city because there isn't a lot of traffic.

Translate the last step here:

⏱ UNIT 6 – FASTER! 🐦

Say:

1. Where do you live?

2. I live in Paris. It is in the north of France.

3. Near my house, there are restaurants.

4. I like my city because it is safe.

5. What is there in your city?

6. In the centre, there is a sports centre.

7. We live in Cardiff. It is in the south of Wales.

8. I like my neighbourhood because one can eat well.

9. In my city, we have many old buildings.

10. Do you like your street?

	Time	Mistakes	Referee's name
1			
2			
3			
4			

UNIT 6 – TRAPDOOR

Dans le centre Dans ma rue Dans ma ville Dans mon quartier Près de chez moi	il y a il n'y a pas d'/de nous avons nous n'avons pas d'/de	un café des restaurants un aquarium un centre commercial un cinéma un club de jeunes un jardin botanique un centre sportif un parc une rue piétonne une patinoire

1. In my city, we have restaurants and a mall.
2. Near my house, there is a park.
3. In my neighbourhood, there isn't an aquarium.
4. In the centre, there is a cinema.
5. On my street, we don't have a youth club.
6. In my city, we have a sports centre.
7. In my neighbourhood, there is a pedestrian street.

	Time 1	Time 2	Time 3	Time 4
Time				
Mistakes				

UNIT 6 – COMMUNICATIVE DRILLS

1	2	3
Do you like your city? Why? - I like my city because there is a youth club. **Where do you live?** - I live in Berlin.	**Do you like your neighbourhood? Why?** - I don't like my neighbourhood because there is a lot of pollution. **What is there in your neighbourhood?** - In my neighbourhood, we have many sports facilities.	**What is there on your street?** - On my street, there aren't many things to do. **Do you like your neighbourhood? Why?** - Yes, I like my neighbourhood because it is safe.
4	**5**	**6**
Do you like your street? Why? - I like my street because it's clean. **Where do you live?** - I live in Madrid. It's in the centre of Spain.	**What is near your house?** - Near my house, there are many cafés. **Where do you live?** - I live in London. It's in the southeast of England.	**Where do you live?** - I live in Rome. **Do you like your city? Why?** - Yes, I like my city because there are many shops.
7	**8**	**9**
Do you like your neighbourhood? Why? - I don't like my neighbourhood because there's a lot of noise. **What is there in your city?** - In my city, there are many shops.	**Where do you live?** - I live in Cardiff. It's in the south of Wales. **What is there in the centre?** - In the centre, there's a park.	**Where do you live?** - I live in Paris. I really like my city. Where do you live? **I live in London. What is there in your city?** - In my city, we have many beautiful streets.

UNIT 6 – COMMUNICATIVE DRILLS
REFEREE CARD

1	2	3
Tu aimes ta ville? Pourquoi? - J'aime ma ville parce qu'il y a un club de jeunes. **Où habites-tu?** - J'habite à Berlin.	**Tu aimes ton quartier? Pourquoi?** - Je n'aime pas mon quartier parce qu'il y a beaucoup de pollution. **Qu'est-ce qu'il y a dans ton quartier?** - Dans mon quartier, nous avons beaucoup d'installations sportives.	**Qu'est-ce qu'il y a dans ta rue?** - Dans ma rue, il n'y a pas beaucoup de choses à faire. **Tu aimes ton quartier? Pourquoi?** - Oui, j'aime mon quartier parce que c'est sûr.
4	5	6
Tu aimes ta rue? Pourquoi? - J'aime ma rue parce que c'est propre. **Où habites-tu?** - J'habite à Madrid. C'est dans le centre de l'Espagne.	**Qu'est-ce qu'il y a près de chez toi?** - Près de chez moi, il y a beaucoup de cafés. **Où habites-tu?** - J'habite à Londres. C'est dans le sud-est de l'Angleterre.	**Où habites-tu?** - J'habite à Rome. **Tu aimes ta ville? Pourquoi?** - Oui, j'aime ma ville parce qu'il y a beaucoup de magasins.
7	8	9
Tu aimes ton quartier? Pourquoi? - Je n'aime pas mon quartier parce qu'il y a beaucoup de bruit. **Qu'est-ce qu'il y a dans ta ville?** - Dans ma ville, il y a beaucoup de magasins.	**Où habites-tu?** - J'habite à Cardiff. C'est dans le sud du Pays de Galles. **Qu'est-ce qu'il y a dans le centre?** - Dans le centre, il y a un parc.	**Où habites-tu?** - J'habite à Paris. J'aime beaucoup ma ville. Où habites-tu? **J'habite à Londres. Qu'est-ce qu'il y a dans ta ville?** - Dans ma ville, nous avons beaucoup de jolies rues.

UNIT 6 – SURVEY

	Comment tu t'appelles? *What is your name?*	Où habites-tu? *Where do you live?*	Qu'est-ce qu'il y a dans ta ville? *What is there in your city?*	Tu aimes ton quartier? *Do you like your neighbourhood?*	Qu'est-ce qu'il y a dans ta rue? *What is there on your street?*	Qu'est-ce qu'il y a dans le centre? *What is there in the centre?*
e.g.	*Je m'appelle Jean.*	*J'habite à Cardiff. C'est dans le sud du Pays de Galles.*	*Dans ma ville, il y a un jardin botanique.*	*Je n'aime pas mon quartier car c'est sale.*	*Dans ma rue, nous avons beaucoup de magasins.*	*Dans le centre, il y a un cinéma et un parc.*
1.						
2.						
3.						
4.						
5.						
6.						
7.						

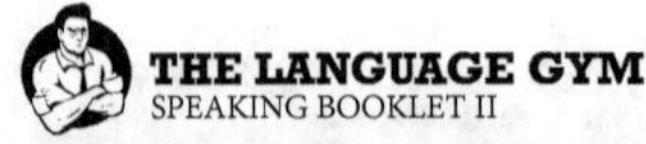

UNIT 6 – ANSWERS

FIND SOMEONE WHO

Find someone who...		Name(s)
1.	...has a pedestrian street in their city centre.	Patricia
2.	...has a shopping centre in their city.	Valérie
3.	...has lots of old buildings in their neighbourhood.	Lionel
4.	...has many things to do in their neighbourhood.	Paul/Carla
5.	...has lots of restaurants on their street.	Michel
6.	...has a sports centre in the city centre.	Pierre/Xavier
7.	...has a youth club on their street.	Alexandre
8.	...doesn't have an aquarium in their city.	Martine/Perrine
9.	...lives near a park.	Raphaël
10.	...lives near a cinema.	Rosanne/Andréa
11.	...has a sports centre in their neighbourhood.	Jean
12.	...has a botanical garden in their city.	Bruno

STAIRCASE TRANSLATION

J'habite à Londres. C'est dans le sud-est de l'Angleterre. Dans mon quartier, il y a beaucoup de choses à faire. J'aime mon quartier parce que c'est propre. Dans ma rue, il y a un parc. Dans le centre, il y a un cinéma et beaucoup de magasins. J'aime ma ville parce qu'il n'y a pas beaucoup de circulation.

FASTER!

REFEREE SOLUTION:

1. Où habites-tu?
2. J'habite à Paris. C'est dans le nord de la France.
3. Près de chez moi, il y a des restaurants.
4. J'aime ma ville parce que c'est sûr.
5. Qu'est-ce qu'il y a dans ta ville?
6. Dans le centre, il y a un centre sportif.
7. Nous habitons à Cardiff. C'est dans le sud du Pays de Galles.
8. J'aime mon quartier parce qu'on peut bien manger.
9. Dans ma ville, nous avons beaucoup de vieux bâtiments.
10. Tu aimes ta rue?

TRAPDOOR

1. Dans ma ville, nous avons des restaurants et un centre commercial.
2. Près de chez moi, il y a un parc.
3. Dans mon quartier, il n'y a pas d'aquarium.
4. Dans le centre, il y a un cinéma.
5. Dans ma rue, nous n'avons pas de club de jeunes.
6. Dans ma ville, nous avons un centre sportif.
7. Dans mon quartier, il y a une rue piétonne.

UNIT 7.
Saying what I can do in my neighbourhood

Qu'est-ce qu'on peut faire dans ton quartier?	*What can one do in your neighbourhood?*
Où peut-on aller?	*Where can one go?*
Qu'est-ce qu'on peut voir ou visiter?	*What can one see or visit?*

Dans mon quartier on peut faire beaucoup de choses. *In my neighbourhood one can do many things.*

J'adore *I love* **J'aime** *I like* **Par exemple, on peut** *For example, one can*	**faire** *to do*	de l'équitation de la natation de la randonnée du footing du sport du tourisme du vélo	*horse riding* *swimming* *hiking* *jogging* *sports* *sightseeing* *cycling*	**à la piscine** *at the swimming pool* **au centre commercial** *in the mall* **au centre sportif** *at the sports centre* **au centre-ville** *in the city centre* **au cinéma de mon quartier** *at my neighbourhood cinema* **au club de tennis** *at the tennis club* **au parc** *in the park* **au stade** *at the stadium* **au terrain de foot (près de chez moi)** *on the football pitch (near my house)* **dans la rue piétonne** *in the pedestrian street* **dans la vieille ville** *in the old town* **dans le quartier des affaires** *in the business part of the city* **dans le quartier touristique** *in the touristy part of the city* **dans les bois** *in the woods* **sur la place** *on the town square*
	jouer *to play*	au foot au golf au rugby	*football* *golf* *rugby*	
	aller *to go*	en boîte de nuit faire les magasins me/se promener	*clubbing* *shopping* *go for a walk*	
	voir *to see*	des concerts des films des matchs de foot des spectacles	*concerts* *films* *football games* *shows*	
	visiter *to visit*	des châteaux des galeries d'art des musées des palais historiques des ruines romaines	*castles* *art galleries* *museums* *historic palaces* *Roman ruins*	

UNIT 7 – FIND SOMEONE WHO – Student Cards

J'aime faire du tourisme dans le centre-ville. **JEAN**	J'aime regarder des films dans le cinéma de mon quartier. **ARTHUR**	J'aime visiter des châteaux dans le quartier touristique. **SARAH**	J'aime visiter des galeries d'art dans le centre-ville. **VALÉRIE**
J'aime jouer au foot au terrain de foot. **RACHEL**	J'aime aller me promener dans la rue piétonne. **GEORGES**	On peut aller faire les magasins au centre commercial. **CHRISTINE**	J'adore jouer au rugby au stade. **PAUL**
J'aime faire de la randonnée dans les bois. **JULIE**	On peut jouer au golf au club de tennis. **LAURE**	J'aime aller à des concerts sur la place. **RAPHAËL**	On peut aller au marché sur la place. **CHLOÉ**
Je vais toujours faire les magasins au centre commercial. **MARCEL**	J'aime faire du tourisme dans le centre-ville. **GUILLAUME**	On peut faire du footing au parc. **NADINE**	J'aime visiter des galeries d'art sur la place. **DENIS**

UNIT 7 – FIND SOMEONE WHO – Student Grid

Qu'est-ce qu'on peut faire dans ton quartier?	*What can one do in your neighbourhood?*
Où peut-on aller?	*Where can one go?*
Qu'est-ce qu'on peut voir ou visiter?	*What can one see or visit?*

Find someone who...		**Name(s)**
1.	...can go to the market at the town square.	
2.	...likes to go for a walk on the pedestrian street.	
3.	...likes to visit art galleries.	
4.	...likes to play football at the football field.	
5.	...loves to visit castles in the touristy part of the city.	
6.	...likes to watch movies at the neighbourhood cinema.	
7.	...plays rugby at the stadium.	
8.	...likes to go to concerts at the town square.	
9.	...likes to do sightseeing in the city centre.	
10.	...can go shopping in the mall.	
11.	...can play golf at the tennis club.	
12.	...goes hiking in the woods.	
13.	...can do jogging in the park.	

UNIT 7 – ORAL PING-PONG – Person A

ENGLISH	FRENCH	ENGLISH	FRENCH
I like to do sightseeing in the city centre.	J'aime faire du tourisme dans le centre-ville.	One can do jogging in the park.	On peut faire du footing dans le parc.
One can swim at the pool at the sports centre.		I like to play football on the football field.	
I like to go for a walk on the pedestrian street.	J'aime aller me promener dans la rue piétonne.	One can go to the market in the town square.	On peut aller au marché sur la place.
I like to visit art galleries in the old town.		I like to visit castles in the tourist area of the city.	
One can do sport at the tennis club.	On peut faire du sport au club de tennis.	I like to swim at the pool at the sports centre.	J'aime faire de la natation dans la piscine au centre sportif.
I like to watch movies in my neighbourhood cinema.		One can do hiking in the woods.	
One can visit museums in the old town.	On peut visiter des musées dans la vieille ville.	I like to go shopping in the mall.	J'aime aller faire les magasins au centre commercial.
I like to go to concerts in the town square.		One can play tennis at the tennis club.	
I love to play rugby at the stadium.	J'adore jouer au rugby au stade.	I like to visit museums in the old town.	J'aime visiter des musées dans la vieille ville.
I like to go clubbing in the touristy part of the city.		I like to see concerts in the park.	

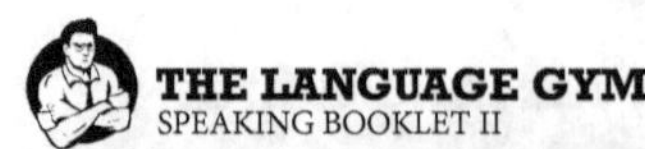

UNIT 7 – ORAL PING-PONG – Person B

ENGLISH	FRENCH	ENGLISH	FRENCH
I like to do sightseeing in the city centre.		One can do jogging in the park.	
One can swim at the pool.	On peut faire de la natation à la piscine.	I like to play football in the football field.	J'aime jouer au foot au terrain de foot.
I like to go for a walk on the pedestrian street.		One can go to the market in the town square.	
I like to visit art galleries in the old town.	J'aime visiter des galeries d'art dans la vieille ville.	I like to visit castles in the tourist area of the city.	J'aime visiter des châteaux dans le quartier touristique.
One can do sport at the tennis club.		I like to swim at the pool at the sports centre.	
I like to watch films in my neighbourhood cinema.	J'aime regarder des films au cinéma de mon quartier.	One can do hiking in the woods.	On peut faire de la randonnée dans les bois.
One can visit museums in the old town.		I like to go shopping in the commercial area of the city.	
I like to go to concerts in the town square.	J'aime aller à des concerts sur la place.	One can play tennis at the tennis club.	On peut jouer au tennis au club de tennis.
I love to play rugby at the stadium.		I like to visit museums in the old town.	
I like to go clubbing in the touristy part of the city.	J'aime aller en boîte dans le quartier touristique.	I like to see concerts in the park.	J'aime voir des concerts au parc.

No Snakes No Ladders

START

1 — I like to visit museums in the touristy part of the city.

2 — One can go to the market in the town square.

3 — I like to play football on the football pitch.

4 — I like to go to my neighbourhood cinema.

5 — One can do hiking in the woods.

6 — What can one see or visit?

7 — Where can one go?

8 — I like to go shopping in the mall.

9 — I like take go for a walk in the pedestrian street.

10 — One can do sport at the tennis club.

11 — I like to watch films in my neighbourhood cinema.

12 — What can one do in your neighbourhood?

13 — One can do jogging in the park.

14 — I like to do sightseeing in the city centre.

15 — I like to visit castles in the touristy part of the city.

16 — In my neighbourhood, one can do many things.

17 — I like to visit art galleries at the old town.

18 — One can watch a football match at the stadium.

19 — I like to play rugby at the stadium.

20 — One can go clubbing in the touristy part of the city.

21 — What can one do in the shopping centre?

22 — I like to go to concerts in the town square.

23 — One can go for a walk in the park.

24 — What can one visit in your neighbourhood?

25 — One can visit historic palaces in the old town.

26 — I like to go to the market in the town square.

27 — One can go shopping at the mall.

28 — I don't like to watch movies in my neighbourhood cinema.

29 — One can visit museums in the city.

30 — I like to play golf in the park.

FINISH

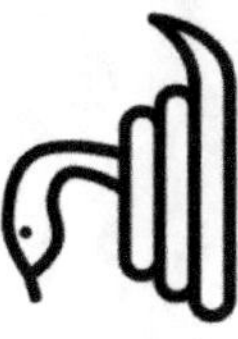

UNIT 7

No Snakes No Ladders

DÉPART

1. J'aime visiter des musées dans le quartier touristique.
2. On peut aller au marché sur la place.
3. J'aime jouer au foot sur le terrain de foot.
4. J'aime aller au cinéma de mon quartier.
5. On peut faire de la randonnée dans les bois.
6. Qu'est-ce qu'on peut voir ou visiter?
7. Où peut-on aller?
8. J'aime aller faire les magasins au centre commercial.
9. J'aime aller me promener dans la rue piétonne.
10. On peut faire du sport au club de tennis.
11. J'aime regarder des films au cinéma de mon quartier.
12. Qu'est-ce qu'on peut faire dans ton quartier?
13. On peut faire du footing au parc.
14. J'aime faire du tourisme dans le centre-ville.
15. J'aime visiter des châteaux dans le quartier touristique.
16. Dans mon quartier, on peut faire beaucoup de choses.
17. J'aime visiter des galeries d'art dans la vieille ville.
18. On peut voir/regarder un match de foot au stade.
19. J'aime jouer au rugby au stade.
20. On peut aller en boîte dans le quartier touristique.
21. Qu'est-ce qu'on peut faire au centre commercial?
22. J'aime aller à des concerts sur la place.
23. On peut se promener au parc.
24. Qu'est-ce qu'on peut visiter dans ton quartier?
25. On peut visiter des palais historiques dans la vieille ville.
26. J'aime aller au marché sur la place.
27. On peut aller faire les magasins au centre commercial.
28. Je n'aime pas regarder des films au cinéma de mon quartier.
29. On peut visiter des musées dans la ville.
30. J'aime jouer au golf au parc.

ARRIVÉE

UNIT 7 – STAIRCASE TRANSLATION

In my neighbourhood, one can do lots of things.

In my neighbourhood, one can do lots of things. For example, one can do sightseeing.

In my neighbourhood, one can do lots of things. For example, one can do sightseeing in the old town.

In my neighbourhood, one can do lots of things. For example, one can do sightseeing in the old town. I like to go for a walk in the woods.

In my neighbourhood, one can do lots of things. For example, one can do sightseeing in the old town. I like to go for a walk in the woods. What can one do in your neighbourhood?

In my neighbourhood, one can do lots of things. For example, one can do sightseeing in the old town. I like to go for a walk in the woods. What can one do in your neighbourhood? I like to go shopping in the mall.

Translate the last step here:

Say:

1. I like to do sport at the sports centre.
2. One can go shopping in the mall.
3. I like to go for a walk on the pedestrian street.
4. I like to go swimming at the pool.
5. One can play football on the football pitch.
6. I like to watch movies in my neighbourhood cinema.
7. One can visit castles in the old town.
8. I like to play golf in the park.
9. I love to go jogging in the woods.
10. One can go sightseeing in the city centre.

	Time	Mistakes	Referee's name
1			
2			
3			
4			

 # UNIT 7 – DETECTIVES & INFORMANTS

DETECTIVES	French	English
Qu'est-ce qu'on peut faire dans ton quartier		
À quoi peut-on jouer dans ta ville?		
Qu'est-ce qu'on peut voir dans ton quartier?		
Où peut-on aller?		
Où aimes-tu aller?		
Qu'est-ce qu'on peut visiter dans ta ville?		
À quoi aimes-tu jouer dans ton quartier?		
Qu'est-ce qu'on peut faire dans le parc?		

INFORMANTS

Dans ma ville, on peut jouer au foot au stade.	On peut faire de la randonnée dans le parc.
Dans mon quartier, j'aime jouer au rugby au centre sportif.	Dans mon quartier, on peut voir des films au cinéma.
Dans mon quartier, on peut faire de l'équitation dans les bois.	On peut aller en boîte sur la place.
J'aime aller au marché dans la vieille ville.	Dans ma ville, on peut visiter des palais historiques dans le centre-ville.

UNIT 7 – COMMUNICATIVE DRILLS

1	2	3
What can one do in your neighbourhood? - In my neighbourhood, one can do sightseeing in the old town. **What can one visit?** - One can visit castles and museums.	**Where can one go?** - One can go to the shopping centre. **What can one do?** - One can go shopping and visit art galleries.	**What do you like to do in your city?** - In my city, I like to watch films in my neighbourhood cinema. And you? **In my neighbourhood, I like to visit the Roman ruins.**

4	5	6
What can one play in your neighbourhood? - One can play golf, but I like to play football in the park. **What can one visit?** - I like to visit the museums in the town square.	**What can you do in your city?** - You can do lots of things. For example, you can do jogging in the pedestrian street. **Where can you go?** - I like to go clubbing in city centre.	**What do you like to do in your city?** - I like to watch football matches in the stadium. And you? **I like to go to concerts in the stadium.**

7	8	9
Where can one go in your neighbourhood? - In my neighbourhood, one can go for a walk in the woods. **What can one do?** - One can do swimming in the swimming pool.	**I like to do horse riding. What can one do in your town?** - I like to play football on the football pitch. I love football and rugby. **I like to play rugby at the park.**	**What can one do in your neighbourhood?** - In my neighbourhood, one can do many things. **What can one watch?** - One can watch a football match at the park.

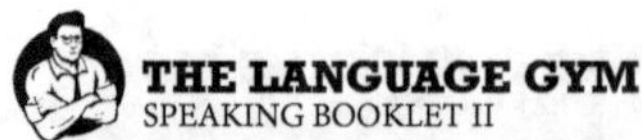

UNIT 7 – COMMUNICATIVE DRILLS
REFEREE CARD

1	2	3
Qu'est-ce qu'on peut faire dans ton quartier? - Dans mon quartier, on peut faire du tourisme dans la vieille ville. **Qu'est-ce qu'on peut visiter?** - On peut visiter des châteaux et des musées.	**Où peut-on aller?** - On peut aller au centre commercial. **Qu'est-ce qu'on peut faire?** - On peut aller faire les magasins et visiter des galeries d'art.	**Qu'est-ce que tu aimes faire dans ta ville?** - Dans ma ville, j'aime voir des films au cinéma de mon quartier. Et toi? **Dans mon quartier, j'aime visiter les ruines romaines.**

4	5	6
À quoi peut-on jouer dans ton quartier? - On peut jouer au golf, mais j'aime jouer au foot au parc. **Qu'est-ce qu'on peut visiter?** - J'aime visiter les musées sur la place.	**Qu'est-ce qu'on peut faire dans ta ville?** - On peut faire beaucoup de choses. Par exemple, on peut faire du footing dans la rue piétonne. **Où peut-on aller?** - J'aime aller en boîte dans le centre-ville.	**Qu'est-ce que tu aimes faire dans ta ville?** - J'aime regarder des matchs de foot au stade. Et toi? **J'aime aller à des concerts au stade.**

7	8	9
Où peut-on aller dans ton quartier? - Dans mon quartier, on peut se promener dans les bois. **Qu'est-ce qu'on peut faire?** - On peut faire de la natation à la piscine.	**J'aime faire de l'équitation. Qu'est-ce qu'on peut faire dans ta ville?** - J'aime jouer au foot sur le terrain de foot. J'adore le foot et le rugby. **J'aime jouer au rugby au parc.**	**Qu'est-ce qu'on peut faire dans ton quartier?** - Dans mon quartier, on peut faire beaucoup de choses. **Qu'est-ce qu'on peut voir?** - On peut voir un match de foot au parc.

UNIT 7 – SURVEY

	Comment tu t'appelles? *What is your name?*	**Qu'est-ce qu'on peut faire au parc?** *What can one do in the park?*	**Où aimes-tu aller?** *Where do you like to go?*	**Qu'est-ce qu'on peut faire dans ton quartier?** *What can one do in your neighbourhood?*	**Qu'est-ce qu'on peut voir dans ton quartier?** *What can one see in your neighbourhood?*	**Qu'est-ce qu'on peut visiter dans ta ville?** *What can one visit in your city?*
e.g.	*Je m'appelle Jean.*	*On peut faire du footing dans le parc.*	*J'aime aller au centre commercial.*	*Dans mon quartier, on peut faire du tourisme dans la vieille ville.*	*On peut voir des films au cinéma.*	*On peut visiter des galeries d'art sur la place.*
1.						
2.						
3.						
4.						
5.						
6.						
7.						

UNIT 7 – ANSWERS

FIND SOMEONE WHO

Find someone who...		Name(s)
1.	...can go to the market at the town square.	**Chloé**
2.	...likes to go for a walk on the pedestrian street.	**Georges**
3.	...likes to visit art galleries.	**Valérie/Denis**
4.	...likes to play football at the football field.	**Rachel**
5.	...loves to visit castles in the touristy part of the city.	**Sarah**
6.	...likes to watch movies at the neighbourhood cinema.	**Arthur**
7.	...plays rugby at the stadium.	**Paul**
8.	...likes to go to concerts at the town square.	**Raphaël**
9.	...likes to do sightseeing in the city centre.	**Jean/Guillaume**
10.	...can go shopping in the mall.	**Marcel/Christine**
11.	...can play golf at the tennis club.	**Laure**
12.	...goes hiking in the woods.	**Julie**
13.	...can do jogging in the park.	**Nadine**

STAIRCASE TRANSLATION

Dans mon quartier, on peut faire beaucoup de choses. Par exemple, on peut faire du tourisme dans la vieille ville. J'aime aller me promener dans les bois. Qu'est-ce qu'on peut faire dans ton quartier? J'aime aller faire les magasins au centre commercial.

FASTER!

REFEREE SOLUTION:
1. J'aime faire du sport au centre sportif.   2. On peut aller faire les magasins au centre commercial.
3. J'aime aller me promener dans la rue piétonne.   4. J'aime faire de la natation à la piscine.
5. On peut jouer au foot au terrain de foot.   6. J'aime voir des films au cinéma de mon quartier.
7. On peut visiter des châteaux dans la vieille ville.   8. J'aime jouer au golf au parc.
9. J'adore faire du footing dans les bois.   10. On peut faire du tourisme dans le centre-ville.

DETECTIVES & INFORMANTS

DETECTIVES	French	English
Qu'est-ce qu'on peut faire dans ton quartier	On peut faire de l'équitation dans les bois.	One can do horse riding in the woods.
À quoi peut-on jouer dans ta ville?	On peut jouer au foot au stade.	One can play football at the stadium.
Qu'est-ce qu'on peut voir dans ton quartier?	On peut voir des films au cinéma de mon quartier.	One can watch films in my neighbourhood cinema.
Où peut-on aller?	On peut aller en boîte sur la place.	One can go clubbing in the town square.
Où aimes-tu aller?	J'aime aller au marché dans la vieille ville.	I like to go to the market in the old town.
Qu'est-ce qu'on peut visiter dans ta ville?	On peut visiter des palais historiques dans le centre-ville.	One can visit historic palaces in the city centre.
À quoi aimes-tu jouer dans ton quartier?	J'aime jouer au rugby au centre sportif.	I like to play rugby at the sports centre.
Qu'est-ce qu'on peut faire dans le parc?	On peut faire de la randonnée dans le parc.	One can go hiking in the park.

UNIT 8.
Describing my street

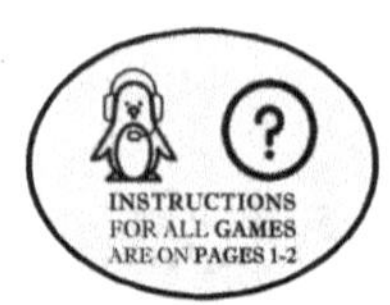

Qu'est-ce qu'il y a dans ta rue?	What is there on your street?
Où est ta maison?	Where is your house?
Quels endroits il y a dans ton quartier?	What places are there in your neighbourhood?

	Masculine nouns		**Feminine nouns**	
Dans ma rue, il y a *On my street, there is*	un arrêt de bus	a bus stop	une bibliothèque	a library
	un bâtiment	a building	une boucherie	a butcher's
	un centre commercial	a shopping mall	une boulangerie	a bakery
	un centre sportif	a sports centre	une église	a church
	un petit parc	a small park	une épicerie	a grocery shop
Près de chez moi, il y a *Near my house, there is*	un restaurant chinois	a chinese restaurant	une gare	a train station
	un supermarché	a supermarket	une mosquée	a mosque
	un terrain de foot	a football pitch	une piscine municipale	a local pool
	un théâtre	a theatre	une synagogue	a synagogue

un magasin de *a ... shop*	**musique** *music*	**sport** *sports*	**vêtements** *clothes*

		à droite — *to the right*	**Fem. nouns**	
Le cinéma *The cinema*		à gauche — *to the left*		bibliothèque
		à dix minutes à pied *a 10 minute walk away*	**de la** *of/from*	boucherie
Ma maison *My house*		à dix minutes en voiture *a 10 minute car ride away*		boulangerie
	est *is*			piscine
Mon immeuble *My block of flats*		à côté — *next to*	**Masc. nouns**	
		près — *near*		centre commercial
		en face — *opposite*	**du** *of/from*	collège — *school*
Mon appartement *My flat*		loin — *far*		musée — *museum*
				terrain de foot *football pitch*

au bout de la rue *at the end of the street*

derrière — *behind*	**la** piscine — *the pool*
devant — *in front of*	**le** stade — *the stadium*

Mon appartement / **Ma maison**	**est**	**entre** *between*	la boucherie / le cinéma	**et**	la piscine / le supermarché

Il n'y a *There is not*	**aucun** *any – sg. masc*	restaurant	**près d'où j'habite** *near where I live*
	aucune *any – sg. fem*	**boutique** *shop*	**dans mon quartier** *in my neighbourhood*
			par ici *around here*

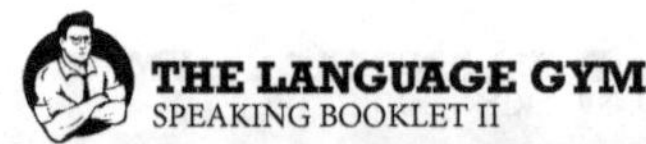

UNIT 8 – FIND SOMEONE WHO – Student Cards

Dans ma rue, il y a une boulangerie et ma maison est à côté de l'église. **JEANNE**	Près de chez moi, il y a une gare. **FRÉDÉRIC**	Dans ma rue, il y a un terrain de foot. **NATHALIE**	Près de chez moi, il y a une bibliothèque. **MARIE**
Près de chez moi, il y a une piscine municipale. **ANTHONY**	Ma maison est à côté d'une église. **DANIEL**	Mon immeuble est en face du collège. **REBECCA**	Ma maison est à dix minutes à pied du parc. **ALEXANDRE**
Dans ma rue, il y a une gare. **RÉMI**	Mon appartement est au bout de la rue. **PHILIPPE**	Mon appartement est derrière le centre commercial. **LÉA**	Mon appartement est entre la piscine et le cinéma. **LUCAS**
Ma maison est loin du terrain de foot. **GEORGES**	Ma maison est entre la boucherie et le supermarché. **SIMON**	Ma maison est près de la bibliothèque. **ROMAIN**	Mon appartement est devant le stade. **MANON**

UNIT 8 – FIND SOMEONE WHO – Student Grid

Qu'est-ce qu'il y a dans ta rue?	*What is there on your street?*
Où est ta maison?	*Where is your house?*
Quels endroits il y a dans ton quartier?	*What places are there in your neighbourhood?*

Find someone who...		Name(s)
1.	...lives in a flat at the end of the street.	
2.	...lives in a house far from the football field.	
3.	...lives in a house between a butcher's and a supermarket.	
4.	...lives near a train station.	
5.	...lives near a local swimming pool.	
6.	...has a football pitch on their street.	
7.	...lives next to a church.	
8.	...lives opposite a school.	
9.	...lives a ten-minute walk away from a park.	
10.	...lives in a flat behind the shopping centre.	
11.	...lives in a flat between the swimming pool and the cinema.	
12.	...lives in a house near the library.	
13.	...lives in a flat in front of the stadium.	

UNIT 8 – ORAL PING-PONG – Person A

ENGLISH	FRENCH	ENGLISH	FRENCH
The cinema is next to the music shop.	Le cinéma est à côté du magasin de musique.	There isn't a sports centre around here.	Il n'y a aucun centre sportif par ici.
My block of flats is opposite the stadium.		My house is between the butcher's and the cinema.	
My flat is to the left of the shopping centre.	Mon appartement est à gauche du centre commercial.	The cinema is behind my block of flats.	Le cinéma est derrière mon immeuble.
My house is far from the football pitch.		My block of flats is in front of the library.	
On my street, there is a small park.	Dans ma rue, il y a un petit parc.	My flat is a ten-minute walk away from the park.	Mon appartement est à dix minutes à pied du parc.
Near my house, there is a bakery.		On my street, there is a supermarket.	
Near my house, there is a football pitch.	Près de chez moi, il y a un terrain de foot.	Near my house, there is a train station.	Près de chez moi, il y a une gare.
There isn't a sports centre near my house.		On my street, there is a shoe shop.	
On my street, there is a church and a bakery.	Dans ma rue, il y a une église et une boulangerie.	There isn't any shop in my neighbourhood.	Il n'y a aucun magasin dans mon quartier.
Near my house, there is a local pool.		My flat is between the cinema and the supermarket.	

UNIT 8 – ORAL PING-PONG – Person B

ENGLISH	FRENCH	ENGLISH	FRENCH
The cinema is next to the music shop.		There isn't a sports centre around here.	
My block of flats is opposite the stadium.	Mon immeuble est en face du stade.	My house is between the butcher's and the cinema.	Ma maison est entre la boucherie et le cinéma.
My flat is to the left of the shopping centre.		The cinema is behind my block of flats.	
My house is far from the football pitch.	Ma maison est loin du terrain de foot.	My block of flats is in front of the library.	Mon immeuble est en face de la bibliothèque.
On my street, there is a small park.		My flat is a ten-minute walk away from the park.	
Near my house, there is a bakery.	Près de chez moi, il y a une boulangerie.	On my street, there is a supermarket.	Dans ma rue, il y a un supermarché.
Near my house, there is a football pitch.		Near my house, there is a train station.	
There isn't a sports centre near my house.	Il n'y a aucun centre sportif près de chez moi.	On my street, there is a shoe shop.	Dans ma rue, il y a un magasin de chaussures.
On my street, there is a church and a bakery.		There isn't any shop in my neighbourhood.	
Near my house, there is a local pool.	Près de chez moi, il y a une piscine municipale.	My flat is between the cinema and the supermarket.	Mon appartement est entre le cinéma et le supermarché.

No Snakes No Ladders

START

FINISH

1. On my street, there is a bakery.

2. On my street, there is a church.

3. My house is close to a bakery.

4. My house is between the butcher's and the cinema.

5. My block of flats is at the end of the street.

6. My flat is near the bakery.

7. What places are there in your neighbourhood?

8. The cinema is to the right of my block of flats.

9. There isn't a sports centre near my house.

10. Near my house, there is a train station.

11. On my street, there is a shopping centre.

12. There isn't any shop in my neighbourhood.

13. My house is opposite the library.

14. My flat is between the cinema and the supermarket.

15. On my street, there is a mosque.

16. Where is your house?

17. There isn't a football pitch around here.

18. My block of flats is behind the museum.

19. My flat is next to the shopping centre.

20. My house is near the football pitch.

21. My house is opposite the stadium.

22. Near my house, there is a supermarket.

23. On my street, there is a butcher's.

24. Near my house, there is a small park.

25. On my street, there is a church.

26. Near my house, there is a local pool.

27. There isn't any shop near my house.

28. What is there on your street?

29. My house is at the end of the street.

30. My house is a ten-minute walk away from the park.

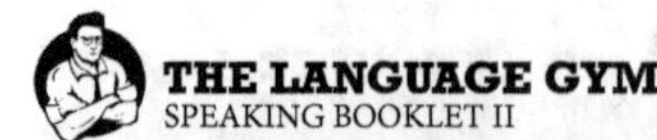

No Snakes No Ladders

DÉPART	
1	Dans ma rue, il y a une boulangerie.
2	Dans ma rue, il y a une église.
3	Ma maison est près d'une boulangerie.
4	Ma maison est entre la boucherie et le cinéma.
5	Mon immeuble est au bout de la rue.
6	Mon appartement est près de la boulangerie.
7	Quels endroits il y a dans ton quartier?
8	Le cinéma est à droite de mon immeuble.
9	Il n'y a aucun centre sportif près de chez moi.
10	Près de chez moi, il y a une gare.
11	Dans ma rue, il y a un centre commercial.
12	Il n'y a aucune boutique dans mon quartier.
13	Ma maison est en face de la bibliothèque.
14	Mon appartement est entre le cinéma et le supermarché.
15	Dans ma rue, il y a une mosquée.
16	Où est ta maison?
17	Il n'y a aucun terrain de foot par ici.
18	Mon immeuble est derrière le musée.
19	Mon appartement est à côté du centre commercial.
20	Ma maison est près du terrain de foot.
21	Ma maison est en face du stade.
22	Près de chez moi, il y a un supermarché.
23	Dans ma rue, il y a une boucherie.
24	Près de chez moi, il y a un petit parc.
25	Dans ma rue, il y a une église.
26	Près de chez moi, il y a une piscine municipale.
27	Il n'y a aucune boutique près de chez moi.
28	Qu'est-ce qu'il y a dans ta rue?
29	Ma maison est au bout de la rue.
30	Ma maison est à dix minutes à pied du parc.
ARRIVÉE	

UNIT 8 – STAIRCASE TRANSLATION

On my street, there is a supermarket and a church.

On my street, there is a supermarket and a church. Near my house, there is a train station.

On my street, there is a supermarket and a church. Near my house, there is a train station. Where is your house?

On my street, there is a supermarket and a church. Near my house, there is a train station. Where is your house? My house is between the cinema and the swimming pool.

On my street, there is a supermarket and a church. Near my house, there is a train station. Where is your house? My house is between the cinema and the swimming pool. There isn't any shop in my neighbourhood.

On my street, there is a supermarket and a church. Near my house, there is a train station. Where is your house? My house is between the cinema and the swimming pool. There isn't any shop in my neighbourhood. What places are there in your neighbourhood?

Translate the last step here:

 UNIT 8 – FASTER! 

Say:

1. Near my house, there is a bakery.

2. On my street, there is a music shop.

3. The cinema is next to the library.

4. What is there on your street?

5. My flat is a ten-minute walk away from the school.

6. My block of flats is behind the football pitch.

7. There isn't a sports centre around here.

8. My house is between the butcher's and the stadium.

9. My flat is between the cinema and the swimming pool.

10. What places are there in your neighbourhood?

	Time	Mistakes	Referee's name
1			
2			
3			
4			

UNIT 8 – FAST & FURIOUS

Focus on prepositions of place

1. Ma maison est ____________ du collège. — *next to*

2. Mon appartement est ____________ le centre commercial. — *in front*

3. Le musée est ____________ le parc et l'épicerie. — *between*

4. La bibliothèque est ____________ la boucherie. — *behind*

5. Le cinéma est ____________ du parc. — *far*

6. Ma maison est ____ ____________ de la boulangerie. — *to the right*

7. Mon immeuble est ____ ____________ du musée. — *opposite*

8. Le restaurant italien est ____________ du magasin de chaussures. — *near*

9. L'arrêt de bus est ____ ____________ de la mosquée. — *to the left*

10. La gare est ____ ________ ____ ____ ____________. — *at the end of the street*

	Time 1	Time 2	Time 3	Time 4
Time				
Mistakes				

UNIT 8 – COMMUNICATIVE DRILLS

1	2	3
Where is your house? - My house is near the music shop. **What is there on your street?** - On my street, there is a supermarket and a shoe shop.	**What places are there in your neighbourhood?** - In my neighbourhood, there is a shopping mall, a small park and a bakery. And you? What is there in your neighbourhood? **Near my house, there is a church and a mosque.**	**My house is between the cinema and the sports centre. Where is your house?** - My house is a ten-minute walk away from the theatre. It is opposite the library.

4	5	6
What is there on your street? - On my street, there is a sports shop and a train station. **Where is the cinema?** - The cinema is next to the school.	**Is there a shop near your house?** - There isn't any shop near my house. However, there is a sports centre on my street.	**Where is your flat?** - My flat is a ten-minute car ride away from the park. **What is there on your street?** - On my street, there is a football pitch and a Chinese restaurant.

7	8	9
Where is your block of flats? - My building is to the left of the museum and opposite the stadium. **Is there a sports centre?** - No, there is not a sports centre in my neighbourhood.	**On my street, there is a small park and a football pitch. What is there on your street?** - On my street, there is a supermarket and a shoe shop. My house is in between the school and the synagogue.	**What places are there in your neighbourhood?** - In my neighbourhood, there is an Italian restaurant. It is behind the shopping mall. **There isn't an Italian restaurant near my house.**

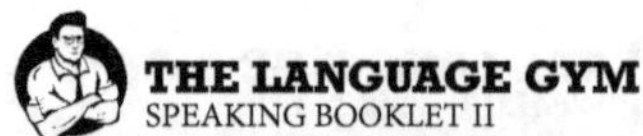

UNIT 8 – COMMUNICATIVE DRILLS
REFEREE CARD

1	2	3
Où est ta maison? - Ma maison est près du magasin de musique. **Qu'est-ce qu'il y a dans ta rue?** - Dans ma rue, il y a un supermarché et un magasin de chaussures.	**Quels endroits il y a dans ton quartier?** - Dans mon quartier, il y a un centre commercial, un petit parc et une boulangerie. Et toi? Qu'est-ce qu'il y a dans ton quartier? **Près de chez moi, il y a une église et une mosquée.**	**Ma maison est entre le cinéma et le centre sportif. Où est ta maison?** - Ma maison est à dix minutes à pied du théâtre. C'est en face de la bibliothèque.
4	**5**	**6**
Qu'est-ce qu'il y a dans ta rue? -Dans ma rue, il y a un magasin de sport et une gare. **Où est le cinéma?** - Le cinéma est à côté du collège.	**Il y a un magasin près de chez toi?** - Il n'y a aucun(e) magasin/boutique près de chez moi. Cependant, il y a un centre sportif dans ma rue.	**Où est ton appartement?** - Mon appartement est à dix minutes en voiture du parc. **Qu'est-ce qu'il y a dans ta rue?** - Dans ma rue, il y a un terrain de foot et un restaurant chinois.
7	**8**	**9**
Où est ton immeuble? - Mon immeuble est à gauche du musée et en face du stade. **Il y a un centre sportif?** - Non, il n'y a aucun centre sportif dans mon quartier.	**Dans ma rue, il y a un petit parc et un terrain de foot. Qu'est-ce qu'il y a dans ta rue?** - Dans ma rue, il y a un supermarché et un magasin de chaussures. Ma maison est entre le collège et la synagogue.	**Quels endroits il y a dans ton quartier?** - Dans mon quartier, il y a un restaurant italien. C'est derrière le centre commercial. **Il n'y a aucun restaurant italien près de chez moi.**

UNIT 8 – SURVEY

	Comment tu t'appelles? *What is your name?*	Qu'est-ce qu'il y a dans ta rue? *What is there on your street?*	Où est ta maison? *Where is your house?*	Quels endroits il y a dans ton quartier? *What places are there in your neighbourhood?*	Où est le cinéma? *Where is the cinema?*	Il y a un centre sportif près de chez toi? *Is there a sports centre near your house?*
e.g.	*Je m'appelle Jean.*	*Dans ma rue, il y a un supermarché.*	*Ma maison est près du parc.*	*Dans mon quartier, il y a une église et un théâtre.*	*Le cinéma est entre la bibliothèque et la boucherie.*	*Il n'y a aucun centre sportif ici.*
1.						
2.						
3.						
4.						
5.						
6.						
7.						

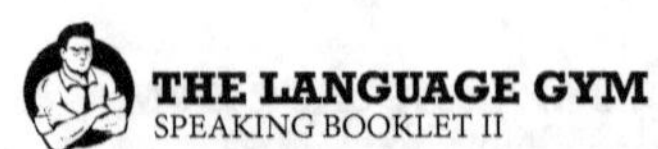

UNIT 8 – ANSWERS

FIND SOMEONE WHO

	Find someone who/whose...	Name(s)
1.	...lives in a flat at the end of the street.	**Philippe**
2.	...lives in a house far from the football field.	**Georges**
3.	...lives in a house between a butcher's and a supermarket.	**Simon**
4.	...lives near a train station.	**Frédéric/Rémi**
5.	...lives near a local swimming pool.	**Anthony**
6.	...has a football pitch on their street.	**Nathalie**
7.	...lives next to a church.	**Jeanne/Daniel**
8.	...lives opposite a school.	**Rebecca**
9.	...lives a ten-minute walk away from a park.	**Alexandre**
10.	...lives in a flat behind the shopping centre.	**Léa**
11.	...lives in a flat between the swimming pool and the cinema.	**Lucas**
12.	...lives in a house near the library.	**Romain/Marie**
13.	...lives in a flat in front of the stadium.	**Manon**

STAIRCASE TRANSLATION

Dans ma rue, il y a un supermarché et une église. Près de chez moi, il y a une gare. Où est ta maison? Ma maison est entre le cinéma et la piscine. Il n'y a aucun(e) magasin/boutique dans mon quartier. Quels endroits il y a dans ton quartier?

FASTER!

REFEREE SOLUTION:

1. Près de chez moi, il y a une boulangerie.
2. Dans ma rue, il y a un magasin de musique.
3. Le cinéma est à côté de la bibliothèque.
4. Qu'est-ce qu'il y a dans ta rue?
5. Mon appartement est à dix minutes à pied du collège.
6. Mon immeuble est derrière le terrain de foot.
7. Il n'y a aucun centre sportif par ici.
8. Ma maison est entre la boucherie et le stade.
9. Mon appartement est entre le cinéma et la piscine.
10. Quels endroits il y a dans ton quartier?

FAST & FURIOUS

1. Ma maison est **près** du collège.
2. Mon appartement est **devant** le centre commercial.
3. Le musée est **entre** le parc et l'épicerie.
4. La bibliothèque est **derrière** la boucherie.
5. Le cinéma est **loin** du parc.
6. Ma maison est **à droite** de la boulangerie.
7. Mon immeuble est **en face** du musée.
8. Le restaurant italien est **près** du magasin de chaussures.
9. L'arrêt de bus est **à gauche** de la mosquée.
10. La gare est **au bout de la rue**.

Combien de pièces il y a dans ta maison?	*How many rooms are there in your house?*
Tu aimes ta maison? Pourquoi?	*Do you like your house? Why?*
Qu'est-ce qu'il y a dans la cuisine / le salon?	*What is there in the kitchen / living room?*

J'habite dans *I live in*	**une maison** *a house*	**dans la banlieue**	*on the outskirts*
	un appartement *a flat*	**à la campagne**	*in the countryside*
Je vis dans *I live in*		**en centre-ville**	*in the city centre*
	un bâtiment *a building*	**sur la côte**	*on the coast*
		à la montagne	*in the mountains*

Dans ma maison *In my house*	**il y a** *there are*	**cinq** *five* **six** *six* **sept** *seven*	**pièces,** *rooms*	**par exemple** *for example* **comme** *such as*	**la chambre de mes parents** *my parents' bedroom*
					ma chambre — *my bedroom*
Dans mon appartement *In my flat*					**une cuisine** — *a kitchen*
					une salle à manger — *a dining room*
					une salle de bains — *a bathroom*
					une salle de jeux — *a games room*
					un salon — *a living room*

il y a aussi *there is also*	**un grenier** *an attic* **un sous-sol** *a basement*	**et** *and*	**un garage** *a garage* **un jardin** *a garden*	

J'aime ma maison car/parce qu' *I like my house because*	**elle est** *it is*	**belle** *beautiful*	
		bien meublée *well-furnished*	
		confortable *comfortable*	
		grande *big*	
		jolie *pretty*	
		lumineuse *well-lit*	
Je n'aime pas ma maison car/parce qu' *I don't like my house because*	**elle n'est pas** *it is not*	**moche** *ugly*	
		petite *small*	
		propre *clean*	
		sale *dirty*	
		spacieuse *spacious*	
		vieille *old*	

J'aime mon appartement car/parce qu' *I like my flat because*	**il est** *it is*	**beau** *beautiful*	**moderne**
		bien meublé	**propre / sale**
		joli	**spacieux**
Je n'aime pas mon appartement car/parce qu' *I don't like my flat because*	**il n'est pas** *it is not*	**lumineux**	**petit**
		moche	**vieux** *old*

Dans la cuisine il y a	Dans le salon il y a	Dans ma chambre il y a	
		une armoire	*a wardrobe*
des chaises *some chairs*	**un canapé** *a sofa*	**un bureau**	*a desk*
un four *an oven*	**un fauteuil** *an armchair*	**une étagère**	*a bookshelf*
un frigo *a fridge*	**une lampe** *a lamp*	**un lit**	*a bed*
un lave-vaisselle *a dishwasher*	**une table basse** *a coffee table*	**un miroir**	*a mirror*
des placards *some cupboards*	**un tapis** *a rug*	**un ordinateur**	*a computer*
une table *a table*	**une télévision** *a TV*	**des rideaux**	*curtains*
		une table de chevet	*a bedside table*

UNIT 9 – FIND SOMEONE WHO – Student Cards

J'habite dans une maison dans la banlieue. **ANNA**	J'aime ma maison car elle est confortable. **ROMAIN**	J'habite dans un bâtiment sur la côte. **ISABELLE**	Dans ma maison, il y a six pièces. Ma pièce préférée, c'est la salle à manger. **FERNAND**
J'habite dans une maison en centre-ville. **XAVIER**	Dans ma maison, il y a sept pièces. Ma pièce préférée, c'est la salle de bains. **LOUIS**	Dans ma maison, il y a six pièces. Ma pièce préférée, c'est la salle à manger. **HÉLÈNE**	Je n'aime pas ma maison car elle est moche. **SONIA**
Dans ma maison, il y a cinq pièces. Par exemple, il y a la chambre de mes parents. **FABIEN**	Dans mon appartement, il y a cinq pièces. Ma pièce préférée, c'est la salle de jeux. **PAULINE**	J'habite dans une maison dans la banlieue. **LAURE**	J'habite dans un appartement en centre-ville. **RAPHAËL**
Ma maison est en centre-ville. **ARTHUR**	Je n'aime pas ma maison car elle n'est pas bien meublée. **PATRICIA**	Je n'aime pas ma maison car elle est vieille. **ROSANNE**	Dans ma maison il y a cinq pièces. Ma pièce préférée, c'est le salon. **JADE**

UNIT 9 – FIND SOMEONE WHO – Student Grid

Combien de pièces il y a dans ta maison?		*How many rooms are there in your house?*	
Tu aimes ta maison? Pourquoi?		*Do you like your house? Why?*	
Où est ta maison?		*Where is your house?*	

Find someone who/whose...		Name(s)
1.	...mentions their bathroom.	
2.	...has six rooms in their house, one being a dining room.	
3.	...mentions a living room.	
4.	...dislikes their house because it is old.	
5.	...lives in a building on the coast.	
6.	...dislikes their house because it is not well furnished.	
7.	...likes their house because it is comfortable.	
8.	...dislikes their house because it is ugly.	
9.	...lives in a house on the outskirts.	
10.	...lives in the city centre.	
11.	...mentions their parents' bedroom.	
12.	...favourite room is their games room.	

UNIT 9 – ORAL PING-PONG – Person A

ENGLISH	FRENCH	ENGLISH	FRENCH
In the kitchen, there is an oven and a table.	Dans la cuisine, il y a un four et une table.	What is there in the living room?	Qu'est-ce qu'il y a dans le salon?
In the kitchen, there is a fridge, a dishwasher, and a table.		I like my house because it's big.	
In my bedroom, there is a bed, a wardrobe, and curtains.	Dans ma chambre, il y a un lit, une armoire et des rideaux.	In the living room, there is a sofa and a television.	Dans le salon, il y a un canapé et une télévision.
I don't like my house because it is dirty.		How many rooms are there in your house?	
In my house, there are five rooms. My favourite room is my parents' bedroom.	Dans ma maison, il y a cinq pièces. Ma pièce préférée, c'est la chambre de mes parents.	In my flat, there are seven rooms. My favourite room is the kitchen.	Dans mon appartement, il y a sept pièces. Ma pièce préférée, c'est la cuisine.
I live in a house in the mountains.		In the kitchen, there is an oven and a fridge.	
I live in a house on the outskirts.	J'habite dans une maison dans la banlieue.	In my bedroom, there is a mirror and a bed.	Dans ma chambre, il y a un miroir et un lit.
How many rooms are there in your house?		Do you like your house?	
In my bedroom, there is a desk and a mirror.	Dans ma chambre, il y a un bureau et un miroir.	I like my flat because it's spacious.	J'aime mon appartement car il est spacieux.
In the living room, there is a rug and a sofa.		I don't like my flat because it's small.	

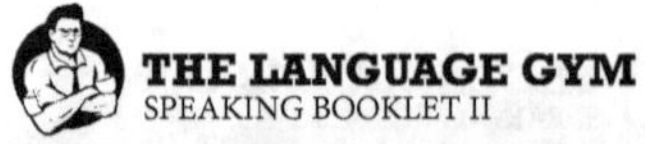

UNIT 9 – ORAL PING-PONG – Person B

ENGLISH	FRENCH	ENGLISH	FRENCH
In the kitchen, there is an oven and a table.		What is there in the living room?	
In the kitchen, there is a fridge, a dishwasher, and a table.	Dans la cuisine, il y a un frigo, un lave-vaisselle et une table.	I like my house because it's big.	J'aime ma maison parce qu'elle est grande.
In my bedroom, there is a bed, a wardrobe, and curtains.		In the living room, there is a sofa and a television.	
I don't like my house because it is dirty.	Je n'aime pas ma maison car elle est sale.	How many rooms are there in your house?	Combien de pièces il y a dans ta maison?
In my house, there are five rooms. My favourite room is my parents' bedroom.		In my flat, there are seven rooms. My favourite room is the kitchen.	
I live in a house in the mountains.	J'habite dans une maison à la montagne.	In the kitchen, there is an oven and a fridge.	Dans la cuisine, il y a un four et un frigo.
I live in a house on the outskirts.		In my bedroom, there is a mirror and a bed.	
How many rooms are there in your house?	Combien de pièces il y a dans ta maison?	Do you like your house?	Tu aimes ta maison?
In my bedroom, there is a desk and a mirror.		I like my flat because it's spacious.	
In the living room, there is a rug and a sofa.	Dans le salon, il y a un tapis et un canapé.	I don't like my flat because it's small.	Je n'aime pas mon appartement car il est petit.

No Snakes No Ladders

START

FINISH

1 — In my bedroom, there is a wardrobe and curtains.

2 — In the living room, there is a coffee table and an armchair.

3 — I like my flat because it is clean.

4 — I don't like my house because it is small.

5 — In my flat, there are six rooms. My favourite room is the dining room.

6 — In my flat, there are six rooms. My favourite room is my bedroom.

7 — I live in a house on the coast.

8 — How many rooms are there in your house?

9 — I live in a house in the city centre.

10 — I like my flat because it is well-lit.

11 — In my bedroom, there is a wardrobe, a bed, and curtains.

12 — In my flat, there are seven rooms. I like my bathroom.

13 — I live in a building in the mountains.

14 — What is there in the kitchen?

15 — I live in a flat on the outskirts.

16 — I live in a flat in the mountains.

17 — I like my house because it's well furnished.

18 — In my flat, there are five rooms. I love my living room.

19 — In my flat, there are five rooms. My favourite room is my bedroom.

20 — In the kitchen, there is a fridge, a table and a chair.

21 — In my house, there are seven rooms. I love my kitchen!

22 — Do you like your flat?

23 — In my bedroom, there is a desk, a mirror, and a computer.

24 — I like my flat because it's well furnished.

25 — I don't like my flat because it's dirty.

26 — I live in a house in the countryside.

27 — Do you like your house?

28 — In the kitchen, there is a fridge and an oven.

29 — I don't like my flat because it's ugly.

30 — I like my house because it's beautiful.

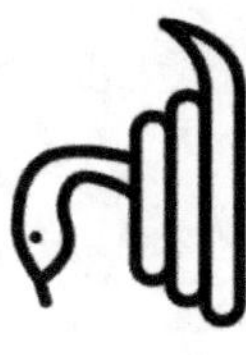

No Snakes No Ladders

DÉPART

1. Dans ma chambre, il y a une armoire et des rideaux.
2. Dans le salon, il y a une table basse et un fauteuil.
3. J'aime mon appartement car il est propre.
4. Je n'aime pas ma maison parce qu'elle est petite.
5. Dans mon appartement, il y a six pièces. Ma pièce préférée est la salle à manger.
6. Dans mon appartement, il y a six pièces. Ma pièce préférée est ma chambre.
7. J'habite dans une maison sur la côte.
8. Combien de pièces il y a dans ta maison?
9. J'habite dans une maison en centre-ville.
10. J'aime mon appartement car il est lumineux.
11. Dans ma chambre, il y a une armoire, un lit et des rideaux.
12. Dans mon appartement, il y a sept pièces. J'aime ma salle de bains.
13. J'habite dans un bâtiment à la montagne.
14. Qu'est-ce qu'il y a dans la cuisine?
15. J'habite dans un appartement dans la banlieue.
16. J'habite dans un appartement à la montagne.
17. J'aime ma maison car elle est bien meublée.
18. Dans mon appartement, il y a cinq pièces. J'adore mon salon.
19. Dans mon appartement, il y a cinq pièces. Ma pièce préférée est ma chambre.
20. Dans la cuisine, il y a un frigo, une table et une chaise.
21. Dans ma maison, il y a sept pièces. J'adore ma cuisine!
22. Tu aimes ton appartement?
23. Dans ma chambre, il y a un bureau, un miroir et un ordinateur.
24. J'aime mon appartement car il est bien meublé.
25. Je n'aime pas mon appartement car il est sale.
26. J'habite dans une maison à la campagne.
27. Tu aimes ta maison?
28. Dans la cuisine, il y a un frigo et un four.
29. Je n'aime pas mon appartement car il est moche.
30. J'aime ma maison car elle est belle.

ARRIVÉE

UNIT 9 – STAIRCASE TRANSLATION

I live in a house in the city centre.

I live in a house in the city centre. In my house, there are 6 rooms.

I live in a house in the city centre. In my house, there are 6 rooms. For example, there is my bedroom and the living room.

I live in a house in the city centre. In my house, there are 6 rooms. For example, there is my bedroom and the living room. There is also an attic and a garden.

I live in a house in the city centre. In my house, there are 6 rooms. For example, there is my bedroom and the living room. There is also an attic and a garden. I like my house because it is beautiful and well-lit. However, it is dirty.

I live in a house in the city centre. In my house, there are 6 rooms. For example, there is my bedroom and the living room. There is also an attic and a garden. I like my house because it is beautiful and well-lit. However, it is dirty. In the kitchen, there is an oven. In my bedroom, there is a bed and a desk.

Translate the last step here:

UNIT 9 – FASTER!

Say:

1. In the living room, there is a television and a sofa.

2. Do you like your house?

3. I live in a flat on the coast.

4. In my house, there are five rooms. My favourite room is the playroom.

5. I like my house because it's well lit.

6. I live in a flat on the outskirts.

7. In my house, there are six rooms. My favourite room is my bedroom.

8. In the kitchen, there is a dishwasher and a chair.

9. In the living room, there is a table and a television.

10. How many rooms are there in your house?

	Time	Mistakes	Referee's name
1			
2			
3			
4			

UNIT 9 – TRAPDOOR

| Dans ma maison

Dans mon appartement | il y a | quatre
cinq
six
sept | pièces. | Ma pièce préférée, c'est

J'aime

J'adore | la chambre de mes parents.
la cuisine.
la salle à manger.
la salle de bains.
la salle de jeux.
le salon. |

1. In my house, there are five rooms. I love my parents' bedroom.

2. In my flat, there are four rooms. My favourite room is the dining room.

3. In my house, there are seven rooms. My favourite room is the games room.

4. In my flat, there are five rooms. I like the bathroom.

5. In my house, there are four rooms. My favourite room is my bedroom.

6. In my flat, there are seven rooms. I love the kitchen.

7. In my house, there are five rooms. My favourite room is the living room.

8. In my flat, there are six rooms. I love the games room.

UNIT 9 – COMMUNICATIVE DRILLS

1	2	3
How many rooms are there in your house? - In my house, there are six rooms. For example, there is my bedroom and a living room. **Where do you live?** - I live in a house in the countryside.	**Do you like your house?** - Yes. I like my house because it is clean and well-furnished. **What is there in your living room?** - In my living room, there is a sofa, a coffee table and a television.	**Where do you live?** - I live in a flat in the city centre. **What is there in your flat?** - In my flat, there are four rooms. My favourite room is the kitchen.

4	5	6
Do you like your house? - I don't like my house because it is old and ugly. **What is there in your bedroom?** - In my bedroom, there is a wardrobe, a mirror and a bed. **Do you like your house?** - Yes, I like my house because it is comfortable.	**What is there in your building?** - In my building, there is a garage and an attic. **Do you live in a flat?** - Yes. I live in a flat on the outskirts. And you? **I live in a house on the coast. I like my house because it is big.**	**Do you like your house?** - Yes. I like my house. **Why?** - I like my house because it is comfortable and clean. What is there in your kitchen? **In my kitchen, there is a fridge, an oven and a dishwasher.**

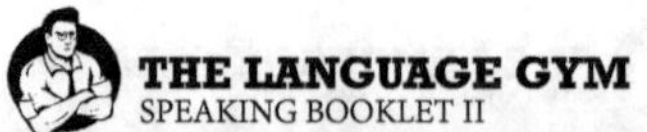

UNIT 9 – COMMUNICATIVE DRILLS
REFEREE CARD

1	2	3
Combien de pièces il y a dans ta maison? - Dans ma maison il y a six pièces. Par exemple, il y a ma chambre et un salon. **Où habites-tu?** - J'habite dans une maison à la campagne.	**Tu aimes ta maison?** -Oui. J'aime ma maison parce qu'elle est propre et bien meublée. **Qu'est-ce qu'il y a dans ton salon?** - Dans mon salon, il y a un canapé, une table basse et une télévision.	**Où habites-tu?** - J'habite dans un appartement en centre-ville. **Qu'est-ce qu'il y a dans ton appartement?** - Dans mon appartement, il y a quatre pièces. Ma pièce préférée, c'est la cuisine.
4	5	6
Tu aimes ta maison? - Je n'aime pas ma maison parce qu'elle est vieille et moche. **Qu'est-ce qu'il y a dans ta chambre?** - Dans ma chambre, il y a une armoire, un miroir et un lit. **Tu aimes ta maison?** - Oui, j'aime ma maison car elle est confortable.	**Qu'est-ce qu'il y a dans ton bâtiment?** - Dans mon bâtiment, il y a un garage et un grenier. **Tu habites dans un appartement?** - Oui. J'habite dans un appartement dans la banlieue. Et toi? **J'habite dans une maison sur la côte. J'aime ma maison parce qu'elle est grande.**	**Tu aimes ta maison?** - Oui. J'aime ma maison. **Pourquoi?** - J'aime ma maison car elle est confortable et propre. Qu'est-ce qu'il y a dans ta cuisine? **Dans ma cuisine, il y a un frigo, un four et un lave-vaisselle.**

UNIT 9 – SURVEY

	Comment tu t'appelles? *What is your name?*	Qu'est-ce qu'il y a dans ta maison? *What is there in your house?*	Combien de pièces il y a dans ta maison? *How many rooms are there in your house?*	Tu aimes ta maison? Pourquoi? *Do you like your house? Why?*	Qu'est-ce qu'il y a dans ta cuisine? *What is there in your kitchen?*	Qu'est-ce qu'il y a dans ta chambre? *What is there in your bedroom?*
e.g.	*Je m'appelle Jean.*	*Dans ma maison, il y a une salle de jeux.*	*Dans ma maison, il y a six pièces.*	*J'aime ma maison car elle est confortable.*	*Dans la cuisine, il y a un four et une table.*	*Dans ma chambre, il y a un lit et un bureau.*
1.						
2.						
3.						
4.						
5.						
6.						
7.						

UNIT 9 – ANSWERS

FIND SOMEONE WHO

	Find someone who/whose...	Name(s)
1.	...mentions their bathroom.	**Louis**
2.	...has six rooms in their house, one being a dining room.	**Fernand/Hélène**
3.	...mentions a living room.	**Jade**
4.	...dislikes their house because it is old.	**Rosanne**
5.	...lives in a building on the coast.	**Isabelle**
6.	...dislikes their house because it is not well furnished.	**Patricia**
7.	...likes their house because it is comfortable.	**Romain**
8.	...dislikes their house because it is ugly.	**Sonia**
9.	...lives in a house on the outskirts.	**Anna/Laure**
10.	...lives in the city centre.	**Xavier/Arthur/Raphaël**
11.	...mentions their parents' bedroom.	**Fabien**
12.	...favourite room is their games room.	**Pauline**

STAIRCASE TRANSLATION

J'habite dans une maison en centre-ville. Dans ma maison, il y a six pièces. Par exemple, il y a ma chambre et le salon. Il y a aussi un grenier et un jardin. J'aime ma maison car elle est jolie et lumineuse. Cependant, elle est sale. Dans la cuisine, il y a un four. Dans ma chambre, il y a un lit et un bureau.

FASTER!

REFEREE SOLUTION:
1. Dans le salon, il y a une télévision et un canapé.
2. Tu aimes ta maison?
3. J'habite dans un appartement sur la côte.
4. Dans ma maison, il y a cinq pièces. Ma pièce préférée, c'est la salle de jeux.
5. J'aime ma maison car elle est lumineuse.
6. J'habite dans un appartement dans la banlieue.
7. Dans ma maison, il y a six pièces. Ma pièce préférée, c'est ma chambre.
8. Dans la cuisine, il y a un lave-vaisselle et une chaise.
9. Dans le salon, il y a une table et une télévision.
10. Combien de pièces il y a dans ta maison?

TRAPDOOR

1. Dans ma maison, il y a cinq pièces. J'adore la chambre de mes parents.
2. Dans mon appartement, il y a quatre pièces. Ma pièce préférée, c'est la salle à manger.
3. Dans ma maison, il y a sept pièces. Ma pièce préférée, c'est la salle de jeux.
4. Dans mon appartement, il y a cinq pièces. J'aime la salle de bains.
5. Dans ma maison, il y a quatre pièces. Ma pièce préférée, c'est ma chambre.
6. Dans mon appartement, il y a sept pièces. J'adore la cuisine.
7. Dans ma maison, il y a cinq pièces. Ma pièce préférée, c'est le salon.
8. Dans mon appartement, il y a six pièces. J'adore la salle de jeux.

UNIT 10.
Saying what I did in my neighbourhood

Où es-tu allé(e) le week-end dernier?		*Where did you go last weekend?*	
Avec qui y es-tu allé(e)?		*Who did you go there with?*	
Qu'est-ce que tu as fait samedi?		*What did you do on Saturday?*	

Avant-hier *The day before yesterday* **Hier** *Yesterday* **Il y a trois jours** *Three days ago* **Le week-end dernier** *Last weekend* **Vendredi dernier** *Last Friday*	**j'ai acheté** *I bought*	**un maillot de foot** **un jeu vidéo** **des vêtements neufs**	*a football shirt* *a videogame* *new clothes*		
	je suis allé(e) *I went*	**à la patinoire** **à un concert** **faire les magasins** **me promener**	*to the skating rink* *to a concert* *shopping* *for a walk*		
	j'ai fait *I did*	**de l'équitation** *horse riding* **de la musculation** *bodybuilding* **de la natation** *swimming*		**de la randonnée** *hiking* **du footing** *jogging* **du tourisme** *sightseeing*	
	j'ai joué *I played*	**au foot** **au golf**		**au rugby** **au tennis**	
		du piano **du violon** *violin*		**de la batterie** *drums* **de la guitare**	
	j'ai regardé *I watched* **j'ai vu** *I saw*	**un spectacle de cirque/danse/magie** *a circus/dance/magic show* **un match de foot** *a football game* **une comédie** *a comedy* **un film d'action/d'horreur** *an action/horror film*			
	j'ai visité *I visited*	**un château** *a castle* **une galerie d'art** *an art gallery* **un musée** *a museum*		**un palais historique** *a historic palace* **des ruines romaines** *some Roman ruins*	

à la *at/to*	**piscine (municipale)**	*the (local) swimming pool*	
au *at/to*	**centre sportif** **cinéma** **club de tennis** **parc** **stade** **terrain de foot**	*the sports centre* *the cinema* *the tennis club* *the park* *the stadium* *the football pitch*	**de mon quartier** *in my neighbourhood* **près de chez moi** *near my house*
dans *in*	**les bois** **le centre commercial** **la rue piétonne**	*the woods* *the shopping mall* *the pedestrian street*	
sur *on*	**la place**	*the town square*	

avec *with*	**mon frère/ma sœur** *my brother/sister* **mon/ma meilleur(e) ami(e)** *my best friend*	**mon/ma petit(e) ami(e)** *my boyfriend/girlfriend* **mon/ma cousin(e)** *my cousin*

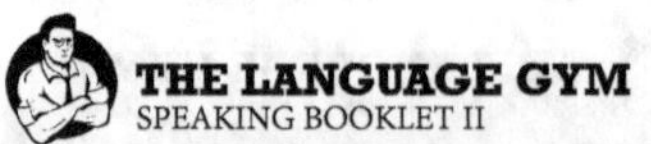

UNIT 10 – FIND SOMEONE WHO – Student Cards

Vendredi dernier, j'ai joué au rugby. **OLIVIA**	Le week-end dernier, j'ai joué au tennis. **DAVID**	Hier, j'ai visité une galerie d'art. **PIERRE**	Hier, je suis allé me promener dans le parc. **GUILLAUME**
Hier je suis allé à un concert sur la place. **SERGE**	Il y a trois jours, j'ai fait de la randonnée. **PAULINE**	Avant-hier, je suis allé à la patinoire. **CHARLES**	Il y a trois jours, j'ai vu un match de foot. **LÉA**
Hier, je suis allée me promener au parc. **SOPHIE**	Avant-hier, j'ai acheté un maillot de foot. **AURÉLIE**	Le week-end dernier, j'ai fait du tourisme. **CARMEN**	Avant-hier, j'ai acheté un jeu vidéo. **ANDRÉ**
Avant-hier, j'ai regardé un film au cinéma. **VICTOR**	Vendredi dernier, j'ai visité un musée. **JEANNE**	Hier, j'ai visité une galerie d'art avec ma mère. **GAËL**	Hier, je suis allé à un concert dans la rue piétonne. **PAUL**

UNIT 10 – FIND SOMEONE WHO – Student Grid

Qu'est-ce que tu as fait vendredi/samedi/le week-end dernier/hier/avant-hier?	
What did you do on Friday/Saturday/last weekend/yesterday/the day before yesterday?	
Find someone who...	**Name(s)**
1. ...visited a museum last Friday.	
2. ...played tennis last weekend.	
3. ...went to a concert yesterday.	
4. ...watched a football match three days ago.	
5. ...went for a walk in the park yesterday.	
6. ...bought a football shirt the day before yesterday.	
7. ...played rugby last Friday.	
8. ...bought a videogame the day before yesterday.	
9. ...visited an art gallery yesterday.	
10. ...did hiking three days ago.	
11. ...went to the skating rink the day before yesterday.	
12. ...watched a movie at the cinema the day before yesterday.	
13. ...did sightseeing last weekend.	

UNIT 10 – ORAL PING-PONG – Person A

ENGLISH	FRENCH	ENGLISH	FRENCH
Yesterday, I visited a museum.	Hier, j'ai visité un musée.	Last weekend, I did sightseeing in the old town.	Le week-end dernier, j'ai fait du tourisme dans la vieille ville.
Three days ago, I saw a magic show.		Three days ago, I played tennis at the tennis club in my neighbourhood.	
Yesterday, I watched a film at the cinema with my girlfriend.	Hier, j'ai regardé un film au cinéma avec ma petite amie.	Last Friday, I visited an art gallery with my best friend (m).	Vendredi dernier, j'ai visité une galerie d'art avec mon meilleur ami.
The day before yesterday, I went for a walk with my mum.		Last weekend, I did hiking in the woods with my cousin (f).	
Yesterday, I bought new clothes at the shopping mall.	Hier, j'ai acheté des vêtements neufs au centre commercial.	Three days ago, I watched a football match at the stadium with my dad.	Il y a trois jours, j'ai regardé un match de foot au stade avec mon père.
Yesterday, I went jogging in the park.		Three days ago, I bought a football shirt at the shopping mall.	
The day before yesterday, I went to the skating rink with my sister.	Avant-hier, je suis allé(e) à la patinoire avec ma sœur.	The day before yesterday, I visited some Roman ruins with my friend (m).	Avant-hier, j'ai visité des ruines romaines avec mon ami.
The day before yesterday, I bought a videogame at the mall.		Last Friday, I went to a concert in the stadium with my sister.	
Last Friday, I played football on the football pitch.	Vendredi dernier, j'ai joué au foot sur le terrain de foot.	Last weekend, I played rugby at the sports centre with my friends.	Le week-end dernier, j'ai joué au rugby au centre sportif avec mes amis.
Three days ago, I visited a historic palace in my neighbourhood.		Yesterday, I saw a circus show in the town square with my family.	

UNIT 10 – ORAL PING-PONG – Person B

ENGLISH	FRENCH	ENGLISH	FRENCH
Yesterday, I visited a museum.		Last weekend, I did sightseeing in the old town.	
Three days ago, I saw a magic show.	Il y a trois jours, j'ai vu un spectacle de magie.	Three days ago, I played tennis at the tennis club in my neighbourhood.	Il y a trois jours, j'ai joué au tennis au club de tennis de mon quartier.
Yesterday, I watched a film at the cinema with my girlfriend.		Last Friday, I visited an art gallery with my best friend (m).	
The day before yesterday, I went for a walk with my mum.	Avant-hier, je suis allé(e) me promener avec ma mère.	Last weekend, I did hiking in the woods with my cousin (f).	Le week-end dernier, j'ai fait de la randonnée dans les bois avec ma cousine.
Yesterday, I bought new clothes at the shopping mall.		Three days ago, I watched a football match at the stadium with my dad.	
Yesterday, I went jogging in the park.	Hier, j'ai fait du footing dans le parc.	Three days ago, I bought a football shirt at the shopping mall.	Il y a trois jours, j'ai acheté un maillot de foot au centre commercial.
The day before yesterday, I went to the skating rink with my sister.		The day before yesterday, I visited some Roman ruins with my friend (m).	
The day before yesterday, I bought a videogame at the mall.	Avant-hier, j'ai acheté un jeu vidéo au centre commercial.	Last Friday, I went to a concert in the stadium with my sister.	Vendredi dernier, je suis allé(e) à un concert au stade avec ma sœur.
Last Friday, I played football on the football pitch.		Last weekend, I played rugby at the sports centre with my friends.	
Three days ago, I visited a historic palace in my neighbourhood.	Il y a trois jours, j'ai visité un palais historique dans mon quartier.	Yesterday, I saw a circus show in the town square with my family.	Hier, j'ai vu un spectacle de cirque sur la place avec ma famille.

No Snakes No Ladders

START

1 — Three days ago, I visited some Roman ruins in the countryside with my sister.

2 — Last weekend, I visited an art gallery with my girlfriend.

3 — Yesterday, I did sightseeing in the old town with my cousin (m).

4 — Yesterday, I bought a football shirt at the mall with my sister.

5 — The day before yesterday, I played football on the football pitch in my neighbourhood.

6 — Last weekend, I went to the park near my house with my dog.

7 — Yesterday, I went to the cinema in the city centre with my best friend (m).

8 — Where did you go last weekend?

9 — Last Friday, I played tennis at the tennis club with my cousin (m).

10 — Yesterday, I watched a film at the cinema with my boyfriend.

11 — The day before yesterday, I watched a football match at the stadium with my sister.

12 — Yesterday, I went shopping at the mall with my sister.

13 — What did you do on Saturday?

14 — Last weekend, I went to the local swimming pool with my brother.

15 — The day before yesterday, I visited a museum in the city centre with my sister.

16 — Three days ago, I visited a castle on the outskirts of the city.

17 — Yesterday, I played golf at the park in my neighbourhood with my father.

18 — Last Friday, I saw a circus show in the park with my cousin (m).

19 — What did you do last Friday?

20 — Yesterday, I did horse riding in the woods with my best friend (f).

21 — Last weekend, I went for a walk on the pedestrian street.

22 — Yesterday, I swam in the local swimming pool with my sister.

23 — Yesterday, I visited an art gallery in the old town with my best friend (m).

24 — Where did you go the day before yesterday?

25 — Yesterday, I bought a videogame at the shopping mall with my brother.

26 — Three days ago, I did jogging in the park near my house with my dog.

27 — Who did you go there with?

28 — Last weekend, I went to the skating rink with my brother.

29 — The day before yesterday, I visited a historic palace in the city centre with my boyfriend.

30 — Yesterday, I bought a football shirt at the mall in my neighbourhood.

FINISH

No Snakes No Ladders

DÉPART	**1** Il y a trois jours, j'ai visité des ruines romaines dans la campagne avec ma sœur.	**2** Le week-end dernier, j'ai visité une galerie d'art avec ma petite amie.	**3** Hier, j'ai fait du tourisme dans la vieille ville avec mon cousin.	**4** Hier, j'ai acheté un maillot de foot au centre commercial avec ma sœur.	**5** Avant-hier, j'ai joué au foot sur le terrain de foot dans mon quartier.	**6** Le week-end dernier, je suis allé(e) au parc près de chez moi avec mon chien.	**7** Hier, je suis allé(e) au cinéma en centre-ville avec mon meilleur ami.
15 Avant-hier, j'ai visité un musée en centre-ville avec ma sœur.	**14** Le week-end dernier, je suis allé(e) à la piscine municipale avec mon frère.	**13** Qu'est-ce que tu as fait samedi?	**12** Hier, je suis allé(e) faire les magasins au centre commercial avec ma sœur.	**11** Avant-hier, j'ai regardé un match de foot au stade avec ma sœur.	**10** Hier, j'ai regardé un film au cinéma avec mon petit ami.	**9** Vendredi dernier, j'ai joué au tennis au club de tennis avec mon cousin.	**8** Où es-tu allé(e) le week-end dernier?
16 Il y a trois jours, j'ai visité un château dans la banlieue de la ville.	**17** Hier, j'ai joué au golf au parc de mon quartier avec mon père.	**18** Vendredi dernier, j'ai vu un spectacle de cirque au parc avec mon cousin.	**19** Qu'est-ce que tu as fait vendredi dernier?	**20** Hier, j'ai fait de l'équitation dans les bois avec ma meilleure amie.	**21** Le week-end dernier, je suis allé(e) me promener dans la rue piétonne.	**22** Hier, j'ai fait de la natation à la piscine municipale avec ma sœur.	**23** Hier, j'ai visité une galerie d'art dans la vieille ville avec mon meilleur ami.
ARRIVÉE	**30** Hier, j'ai acheté un maillot de foot au centre commercial de mon quartier.	**29** Avant-hier, j'ai visité un palais historique en centre-ville avec mon petit ami.	**28** Le week-end dernier, je suis allé(e) à la patinoire avec mon frère.	**27** Avec qui y es-tu allé(e)?	**26.** Il y a trois jours, j'ai fait du footing au parc près de chez moi avec mon chien.	**25** Hier, j'ai acheté un jeu vidéo au centre commercial avec mon frère.	**24** Où es-tu allé(e) avant-hier?

UNIT 10 – STAIRCASE TRANSLATION

Three days ago, I bought new clothes and a videogame.

Three days ago, I bought new clothes and a videogame in the mall near my house.

Three days ago, I bought new clothes and a videogame in the mall near my house with my best friend (f) and my brother.

Three days ago, I bought new clothes and a videogame in the mall near my house with my best friend (f) and my brother. What did you do last Friday?

Three days ago, I bought new clothes and a videogame in the mall near my house with my best friend (f) and my brother. What did you do last Friday? Last weekend, I played tennis at the sports centre.

Three days ago, I bought new clothes and a videogame in the mall near my house with my best friend (f) and my brother. What did you do last Friday? Last weekend, I played tennis at the sports centre near my house with my girlfriend.

Translate the last step here:

⏱ UNIT 10 – FASTER! 🐦

Say:

1. Yesterday, I went for a walk in the park.

2. Three days ago, I watched a film at the cinema.

3. Last weekend, I visited the castle in the old town.

4. The day before yesterday, I played football on the football pitch near my house.

5. Last Friday, I did jogging in the woods near my house with my brother.

6. Yesterday, I went to a dance show in the town square of my neighbourhood with my girlfriend.

7. Where did you go last Friday?

8. Last Saturday, I bought a football shirt in the shopping mall near my house with my cousin (m).

	Time	Mistakes	Referee's name
1			
2			
3			
4			

UNIT 10 – THINGS IN COMMON

Write your own answers to the questions then interview four friends and make a note of what things you have in common.

	Moi *(Your own answer)*	1	2	3
Où es-tu allé(e) le week-end dernier?				
Qu'est-ce que tu as fait vendredi dernier?				
Qu'est-ce que tu as fait samedi dernier?				
Où es-tu allé(e) hier?				
À quoi as-tu joué la semaine dernière?				
Qu'est-ce que tu as visité hier?				
Qu'est-ce que tu as regardé avant-hier?				

UNIT 10 – COMMUNICATIVE DRILLS

1	2	3
Where did you go yesterday? - Yesterday, I went to the sports centre near my house. **Who did you go there with?** - I went there with my brother and my sister. The day before yesterday, I visited an art gallery.	**What did you do on Saturday?** - On Saturday, I went for a walk in the park with my best friend (f). Where did you go on Saturday? **Last Saturday, I visited a museum in the city centre.**	**What did you do last weekend?** - Last weekend, I saw a football match at the stadium, I did swimming at the pool and I went shopping. And you? **Last Saturday, I visited a historic palace in the old town with my girlfriend.**
4	5	6
What did you do three days ago? - Three days ago, I did hiking in the woods in my neighbourhood. **Who did you go there with?** - I went there with my boyfriend and my cousin (f).	**What did you do last Friday?** - Last Friday, I watched a film in my neighbourhood cinema with my best friend (m). And you? **Last Friday, I played golf at the park with my brother and I did jogging.**	**Where did you go last Saturday?** - Last Saturday, I went shopping on the pedestrian street near my house. **Who did you go there with?** - I went there with my girlfriend and my brother.

UNIT 10 – COMMUNICATIVE DRILLS
REFEREE CARD

1	2	3
Où es-tu allé(e) hier? - Hier, je suis allé(e) au centre sportif près de chez moi. **Avec qui y es-tu allé(e)?** - J'y suis allé(e) avec mon frère et ma sœur. Avant-hier, j'ai visité une galerie d'art.	**Qu'est-ce que tu as fait samedi?** - Samedi, je suis allé(e) me promener au parc avec ma meilleure amie. Où es-tu allé(e) samedi? **Samedi dernier, j'ai visité un musée en centre-ville.**	**Qu'est-ce que tu as fait le week-end dernier?** - Le week-end dernier, j'ai vu un match de foot au stade, j'ai fait de la natation à la piscine et je suis allé(e) faire les magasins. Et toi? **Samedi dernier, j'ai visité un palais historique dans la vieille ville avec ma petite amie.**
4	**5**	**6**
Qu'est-ce que tu as fait il y a trois jours? - Il y a trois jours, j'ai fait de la randonnée dans les bois de mon quartier. **Avec qui y es-tu allé(e)?** - J'y suis allé(e) avec mon petit ami et ma cousine.	**Qu'est-ce que tu as fait vendredi dernier?** - Vendredi dernier, j'ai regardé un film au cinéma de mon quartier avec mon meilleur ami. Et toi? **Vendredi dernier, j'ai joué au golf au parc avec mon frère et j'ai fait du footing.**	**Où es-tu allé(e) samedi dernier?** - Samedi dernier, je suis allé(e) faire les magasins dans la rue piétonne près de chez moi. **Avec qui y es-tu allé(e)?** - J'y suis allé(e) avec ma petite amie et mon frère.

UNIT 10 – SURVEY

	Comment tu t'appelles? *What is your name?*	Où es-tu allé(e) le week-end dernier? *Where did you go last weekend?*	Qu'est-ce que tu as fait vendredi dernier? *What did you do last Friday?*	À quoi as-tu joué hier? *What did you play yesterday?*	Qu'est-ce que tu as visité hier? *What did you visit yesterday?*	Qu'est-ce que tu as regardé le week-end dernier? *What did you watch last weekend?*
e.g.	*Je m'appelle Jean.*	*Le week-end dernier, je suis allé(e) au parc.*	*Vendredi dernier, j'ai acheté des vêtements neufs.*	*Hier, j'ai joué au tennis au club de tennis.*	*Hier, j'ai visité une galerie d'art.*	*Le week-end dernier, j'ai regardé un film au cinéma.*
1.						
2.						
3.						
4.						
5.						
6.						
7.						

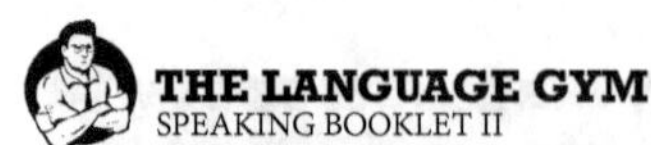

UNIT 10 – ANSWERS

FIND SOMEONE WHO

	Find someone who...	Name(s)
1.	...visited a museum last Friday.	**Jeanne**
2.	...played tennis last weekend.	**David**
3.	...went to a concert yesterday.	**Serge/Paul**
4.	...watched a football match three days ago.	**Léa**
5.	...went for a walk in the park yesterday.	**Guillaume/Sophie**
6.	...bought a football shirt the day before yesterday.	**Aurélie**
7.	...played rugby last Friday.	**Olivia**
8.	...bought a videogame the day before yesterday.	**André**
9.	...visited an art gallery yesterday.	**Pierre/Gaël**
10.	...did hiking three days ago.	**Pauline**
11.	...went to the skating rink the day before yesterday.	**Charles**
12.	...watched a movie at the cinema the day before yesterday.	**Victor**
13.	...did sightseeing last weekend.	**Carmen**

STAIRCASE TRANSLATION

Il y a trois jours, j'ai acheté des vêtements neufs et un jeu vidéo au centre commercial près de chez moi avec ma meilleure amie et mon frère. Qu'est-ce que tu as fait vendredi dernier? Le week-end dernier, j'ai joué au tennis au centre sportif près de chez moi avec ma petite amie.

FASTER!

REFEREE SOLUTION:

1. Hier, je suis allé(e) me promener au parc.

2. Il y a trois jours, j'ai regardé un film au cinéma.

3. Le week-end dernier, j'ai visité le château dans la vieille ville.

4. Avant-hier, j'ai joué au foot au terrain de foot près de chez moi.

5. Vendredi dernier, j'ai fait du footing dans les bois près de chez moi avec mon frère.

6. Hier, je suis allé(e) à un spectacle de danse sur la place de mon quartier avec ma petite amie.

7. Où es-tu allé(e) vendredi dernier?

8. Samedi dernier, j'ai acheté un maillot de foot au centre commercial près de chez moi avec mon cousin.

THINGS IN COMMON

Students give their own answers to the questions and make a note of which students they have things in common with.

UNIT 11.
Saying what I did & am going to do at the weekend

Qu'est-ce que tu as fait le week-end dernier?	*What did you do last weekend?*
C'était comment?	*How was it?*
Qu'est-ce que tu vas faire le week-end prochain?	*What are you going to do next weekend?*
Qu'est-ce que va faire ton frère/ta sœur?	*What is your brother/sister going to do?*

Le week-end prochain *Next weekend*	je vais *I am going*	**faire** *to do*	du cheval / mes devoirs / du sport / du vélo	*horse riding / my homework / sports / cycling*
	ma sœur va *my sister is going*	**aller** *to go*	à une fête / au centre commercial / faire des courses	*to a party / to the mall / shopping*
Samedi prochain *Next Saturday*	mon frère et moi allons *my brother and I are going*	**jouer** *to play*	au basket / sur mon ordinateur	*basketball / on my computer*
Dimanche prochain *Next Sunday*	mes parents vont *my parents are going*	**voir** *to see*	un concert / un match de foot / un film	*a concert / a football match / a film*

Ce sera *It will be*	**assez** *quite* **un peu** *a bit* **très** *very*	**ennuyeux** *boring*
Ce ne sera pas du tout *It won't be … at all*		**amusant** *fun* **intéressant** *interesting*

Le week-end dernier *Last weekend*	**je suis allé(e)** *I went* **nous sommes allé(e)s** *we went*	**chez un(e) ami(e)** *to a friend's house* **au stade** *to the stadium*
	j'ai fait *I did* **nous avons fait** *we did*	du cheval *horseriding* mes devoirs *my homework* nos devoirs *our homework* du sport *sports* du vélo *cycling*
Vendredi dernier *Last Friday*	**j'ai joué** *I played* **nous avons joué** *we played*	aux jeux vidéo *video games* sur mon ordinateur *on my computer* sur notre ordinateur *on our computer*
Dimanche dernier *Last Sunday*	**j'ai vu** *I saw* **nous avons vu** *we saw*	un concert un film un match de foot

Mon ami(e) et moi, nous sommes allé(e)s...	*My friend and I (we) went...*
Mon ami(e) et moi, nous avons fait/joué/vu...	*My friend and I (we) did/played/saw...*

C'était *It was*	**assez** *quite*	**un peu** *a bit*	**très** *very*	**cool** *cool*
Ce n'était pas … du tout *It was not … at all*				**nul** *rubbish* **épuisant** *exhausting* **passionnant** *exciting*

UNIT 11 – FIND SOMEONE WHO – Student Cards

Le week-end dernier, nous avons vu un match de foot. **MYRIAM**	Samedi prochain, ma sœur va aller à une fête. **JULES**	Dimanche prochain, mes parents vont aller à une fête. **LUCAS**	Le week-end dernier, nous avons regardé un film à la maison. **JÉRÔME**
Vendredi dernier, j'ai joué de la guitare. **ANTHONY**	Dimanche prochain, mes parents vont faire du sport. **CÉDRIC**	Dimanche dernier, j'ai fait mes devoirs dans le salon. **GEORGES**	Vendredi dernier, mon ami et moi avons joué au foot. **DAVID**
Dimanche dernier, nous avons joué aux jeux vidéo. **FRANÇOIS**	Vendredi dernier, je suis allé chez un ami. **JEAN**	Dimanche dernier, nous avons joué du piano. **CÉCILE**	Le week-end prochain, mon frère et moi allons voir un match de foot. **SAMUEL**
Le week-end prochain, je vais aller au centre commercial. **BRUNO**	Dimanche dernier, j'ai fait mes devoirs. **ALBANE**	Vendredi dernier, j'ai joué de la guitare dans ma chambre. **HÉLÈNE**	Le week-end prochain, je vais aller au centre commercial. **STÉPHANE**

UNIT 11 – FIND SOMEONE WHO – Student Grid

Qu'est-ce que tu as fait le week-end dernier?	*What did you do last weekend?*
Qu'est-ce que tu as fait vendredi dernier?	*What did you do last Friday?*
Qu'est-ce que tu vas faire le week-end prochain?	*What are you going to do next weekend?*

Find someone who...		**Name(s)**
1.	...has parents who are going to do sport next Sunday.	
2.	...has a sister who is going to a party next Saturday.	
3.	...played the piano last Sunday.	
4.	...played the guitar last Friday.	
5.	...played videogames last Sunday.	
6.	...is going to watch a football match next weekend.	
7.	...went to their friend's house last Friday.	
8.	...watched a movie at home last weekend.	
9.	...is going to the shopping mall next weekend.	
10.	...did homework last Sunday.	
11.	...has parents who are going to a party next Sunday.	
12.	...played football last Friday.	
13.	...watched a football match last weekend.	

UNIT 11 – ORAL PING-PONG – Person A

ENGLISH	FRENCH	ENGLISH	FRENCH
Last weekend, we went to the stadium.	Le week-end dernier, nous sommes allés au stade.	**What are you going to do next weekend?**	Qu'est-ce que tu vas faire le week-end prochain?
Last Friday, I played videogames on my computer.		**Next Sunday, my sister is going to play basketball.**	
It wasn't fun at all.	Ce n'était pas amusant du tout.	**Next weekend, I'm going to see a movie.**	Le week-end prochain, je vais voir un fim.
Next weekend, I'm going to play basketball.		**It was a bit boring.**	
Next Saturday, I'm going to do my homework.	Samedi prochain, je vais faire mes devoirs.	**Next weekend, my brother and I are going to watch a football match.**	Le week-end prochain, mon frère et moi allons voir un match de foot.
What did you do last weekend?		**Next Sunday, my parents are going to a party.**	
Next Sunday, my sister is going to do sport.	Dimanche prochain, ma sœur va faire du sport.	**Last Friday, my friends and I did sport.**	Vendredi dernier, mes amis et moi avons fait du sport.
Last Friday, we went to the stadium.		**Last Sunday, we went to my friend's house.**	
Last weekend, I did my homework.	Le week-end dernier, j'ai fait mes devoirs.	**It won't be interesting at all.**	Ce ne sera pas intéressant du tout.
It will be quite exhausting.		**Last weekend, we did sport.**	

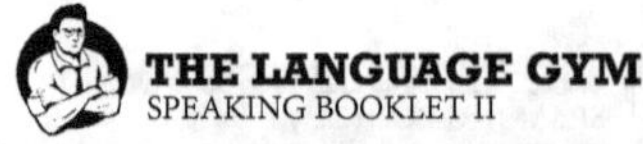

UNIT 11 – ORAL PING-PONG – Person B

ENGLISH	FRENCH	ENGLISH	FRENCH
Last weekend, we went to the stadium.		**What are you going to do next weekend?**	
Last Friday, I played videogames on my computer.	Vendredi dernier, j'ai joué aux jeux vidéo sur mon ordinateur.	**Next Sunday, my sister is going to play basketball.**	Dimanche prochain, ma sœur va jouer au basket.
It wasn't fun at all.		**Next weekend, I'm going to see a movie.**	
Next weekend, I'm going to play basketball.	Le week-end prochain, je vais jouer au basket.	**It was a bit boring.**	C'était un peu ennuyeux.
Next Saturday, I'm going to do homework.		**Next weekend, my brother and I are going to watch a football match.**	
What did you do last weekend?	Qu'est-ce que tu as fait le week-end dernier?	**Next Sunday, my parents are going to a party.**	Le week-end prochain, mes parents vont aller à une fête.
Next Sunday, my sister is going to do sport.		**Last Friday, my friends and I did sport.**	
Last Friday, we went to the stadium.	Vendredi dernier, nous sommes allés au stade.	**Last Sunday, we went to my friend's house.**	Dimanche dernier, nous sommes allés chez un ami.
Last weekend, I did my homework.		**It won't be interesting at all.**	
It will be quite exhausting.	Ce sera assez épuisant.	**Last weekend, we did sport.**	Le week-end dernier, nous avons fait du sport.

No Snakes No Ladders

START

1 — Last Sunday, I played guitar.

2 — Last weekend, we played football.

3 — Next Sunday, my sister is going to play piano.

4 — Next Saturday, my brother and I are going to play basketball.

5 — Next weekend, I'm going to go to the shopping mall.

6 — It wasn't fun at all.

7 — What did you do last weekend?

8 — Next Sunday, my parents are going shopping.

9 — Last weekend, we went to the stadium.

10 — Next Sunday, we're going to go to a party.

11 — Last Sunday, I saw a football match.

12 — It will be quite interesting.

13 — Next weekend, I am going to do my homework.

14 — Last Friday, my friends and I did sport.

15 — Next Saturday, we're going to play the drums.

16 — Last Friday, I did my homework.

17 — It will be very fun.

18 — Last Friday, I played videogames on my computer.

19 — Last Sunday, I saw a movie.

20 — Next Sunday, I'm going to watch a movie at the cinema.

21 — How was it?

22 — Next weekend, we're going to go to a concert.

23 — Next Saturday, my parents are going to do sport.

24 — Last Sunday, we played videogames on my computer.

25 — It was very interesting.

26 — Next Saturday, I'm going to see a football match.

27 — Last Saturday, we did sport.

28 — Last Sunday, I went to my friend's house.

29 — What is your brother going to do?

30 — Next Saturday, we're going to see a football match.

FINISH

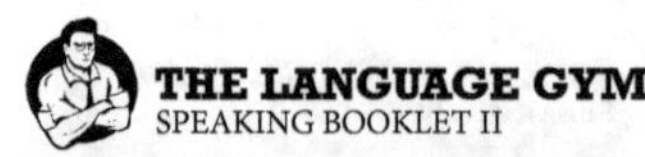

No Snakes No Ladders

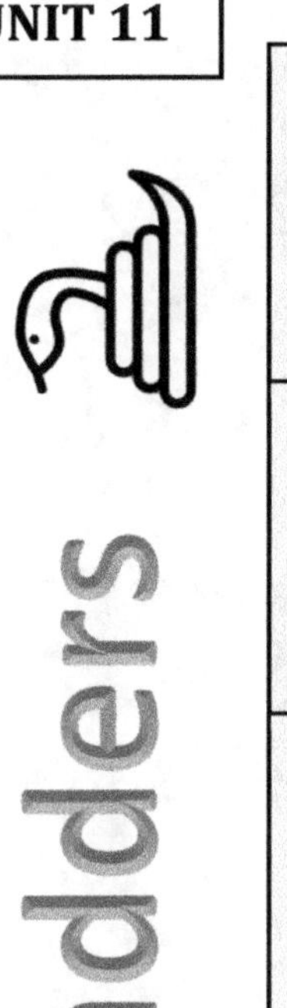

7 Qu'est-ce que tu as fait le week-end dernier?	**8** Dimanche prochain, mes parents vont aller faire des courses.	**23** Samedi prochain, mes parents vont faire du sport.	**24** Dimanche dernier, nous avons joué aux jeux vidéo sur mon ordinateur.
6 Ce n'était pas amusant du tout.	**9** Le week-end dernier, nous sommes allés au stade.	**22** Le week-end prochain, nous allons aller à un concert.	**25** C'était très intéressant.
5 Le week-end prochain, je vais aller au centre commercial.	**10** Dimanche prochain, nous allons aller à une fête.	**21** C'était comment?	**26** Samedi prochain, je vais voir un match de foot.
4 Samedi prochain, mon frère et moi allons jouer au basket.	**11** Dimanche dernier, j'ai vu un match de foot.	**20** Dimanche prochain, je vais aller voir un film au cinéma.	**27** Samedi dernier, nous avons fait du sport.
3 Dimanche prochain, ma sœur va jouer du piano.	**12** Ce sera assez intéressant.	**19** Dimanche dernier, j'ai vu un film.	**28** Dimanche dernier, je suis allé(e) chez mon ami(e).
2 Le week-end dernier, nous avons joué au foot.	**13** Le week-end prochain, je vais faire mes devoirs.	**18** Vendredi dernier, j'ai joué aux jeux vidéo sur mon ordinateur.	**29** Qu'est-ce que va faire ton frère?
1 Dimanche dernier, j'ai joué de la guitare.	**14** Vendredi dernier, mes amis et moi avons fait du sport.	**17** Ce sera très amusant.	**30** Samedi prochain, nous allons voir un match de foot.
DÉPART	**15** Samedi prochain, nous allons jouer de la batterie.	**16** Vendredi dernier, j'ai fait mes devoirs.	**ARRIVÉE**

UNIT 11 – STAIRCASE TRANSLATION

Last weekend, I saw a football match.

Last weekend, I saw a football match. It was quite fun.

Last weekend, I saw a football match. It was quite fun. Next Saturday, my brother and I are going to go to a party.

Last weekend, I saw a football match. It was quite fun. Next Saturday, my brother and I are going to go to a party. Next Sunday, I'm going to do my homework.

Last weekend, I saw a football match. It was quite fun. Next Saturday, my brother and I are going to go to a party. Next Sunday, I'm going to do my homework. It will be very exhausting.

Last weekend, I saw a football match. It was quite fun. Next Saturday, my brother and I are going to go to a party. Next Sunday, I'm going to do my homework. It will be very exhausting. What are you going to do next weekend ?

Translate the last step here :

⏱ UNIT 11 – FASTER! 🚀

Say:

1. Last weekend, I did sport.

2. Next Saturday, I'm going to go shopping.

3. It will be quite interesting.

4. Last Sunday, we saw a football match.

5. Last Friday, my friend and I played videogames.

6. Next Saturday, my sister is going to go to a concert.

7. It was not fun at all.

8. What are you going to do this weekend?

9. It will be very fun and interesting.

10. Next Sunday, my parents are going to go to a party.

	Time	Mistakes	Referee's name
1			
2			
3			
4			

UNIT 11 – FLUENCY CARDS

Next weekend, I...		
Last Sunday, we...		
Last Friday, my friend and I...		
Next Saturday, I...		
Last Sunday, my sister...		
Next weekend, I...		

	Time	Mistakes
1		
2		
3		
4		

UNIT 11 – COMMUNICATIVE DRILLS

1	2	3
What did you do last weekend? - Last weekend, I went to my friend's house. **How was it?** - It was quite fun. It wasn't boring at all.	**What are you going to do next Saturday?** - Next Saturday, my brother and I are going to play basketball. It will be very exhausting. What are you going to do next weekend? **I am going to do my homework.**	**What is your brother going to do next Saturday?** - Next Saturday, my brother is going to watch a football match. Do you have a brother? **Yes, I have a brother. Next Saturday, my brother and I are going to watch a film.**

4	5	6
What did you do with your family last Sunday? - Last Sunday, we went to the stadium. **How was it?** - We watched a football match and it was very cool. Next Sunday, we are going to play basketball.	**What are you going to do next Sunday?** - Next Sunday, my parents and I are going to go to the shopping mall. We are going to go shopping and watch a film. And you? **Next Sunday, I are going to do my homework with my sister. It will be very boring.**	**What are you going to do next weekend?** - Next weekend, I am going to play the drums and I am going to go to a concert. **What is your sister going to do?** - My sister is going to go shopping.

7	8	9
Last weekend, my friend and I played videogames. What did you do last weekend? - Last weekend, I did sport. It was quite exhausting. What are you going to do next Friday? **Next Friday, my sister and I are going to go to a party. It will be cool!**	**Last Friday, I went to a party.** - How was it? **It was not fun at all. What are you going to do next weekend?** - Next Saturday, I am going to do sport. Next Sunday, I'm going to go to a concert. It will be exhausting!	**What is your sister going to do next Friday?** - Next Friday, my sister is going to go to the shopping mall. She is going to go shopping. And you? **Next Friday, I'm going to do hiking because I went shopping last Saturday.**

UNIT 11 – COMMUNICATIVE DRILLS REFEREE CARD

1	2	3
Qu'est-ce que tu as fait le week-end dernier? - Le week-end dernier, je suis allé chez mon ami. **C'était comment?** - C'était assez amusant. Ce n'était pas ennuyeux du tout.	**Qu'est-ce que tu vas faire samedi prochain?** - Samedi prochain, mon frère et moi allons jouer au basket. Ce sera très épuisant. Qu'est-ce que tu vas faire le week-end prochain? **Je vais faire mes devoirs.**	**Qu'est-ce que va faire ton frère samedi prochain?** - Samedi prochain, mon frère va voir un match de foot. Tu as un frère? **Oui, j'ai un frère. Samedi prochain, mon frère et moi allons voir un film.**
4	**5**	**6**
Qu'est-ce que tu as fait avec ta famille dimanche dernier? - Dimanche dernier, nous sommes allés au stade. **C'était comment?** - Nous avons vu un match de foot et c'était très cool. Dimanche prochain, nous allons jouer au basket.	**Qu'est-ce que tu vas faire dimanche prochain?** - Dimanche prochain, mes parents et moi allons aller au centre commercial. Nous allons aller faire des courses et voir un film. Et toi? **Dimanche prochain, je vais faire mes devoirs avec ma sœur. Ce sera très ennuyeux.**	**Qu'est-ce que tu vas faire le week-end prochain?** - Le week-end prochain, je vais jouer de la batterie et je vais aller à un concert. **Qu'est-ce que va faire ta sœur?** Ma sœur va aller faire des courses.
7	**8**	**9**
Le week-end dernier, mon ami et moi avons joué aux jeux vidéo. Qu'est-ce que tu as fait le week-end dernier? - Le week-end dernier, j'ai fait du sport. C'était assez épuisant. Qu'est-ce que tu vas faire vendredi prochain? **Vendredi prochain, ma sœur et moi allons aller à une fête. Ce sera cool!**	**Vendredi dernier, je suis allè à une fête.** - C'était comment? **Ce n'était pas amusant du tout. Qu'est-ce que tu vas faire le week-end prochain?** - Samedi prochain, je vais faire du sport. Dimanche prochain, je vais aller à un concert. Ce sera épuisant!	**Qu'est-ce que va faire ta sœur vendredi prochain?** - Vendredi prochain, ma sœur va aller au centre commercial. Elle va aller faire les courses. Et toi? **Vendredi prochain, je vais faire de la randonnée parce que je suis allé(e) faire les courses samedi dernier.**

UNIT 11 – SURVEY

	Comment tu t'appelles? *What is your name?*	Qu'est-ce que tu as fait le week-end dernier? *What did you do last weekend?*	C'était comment? *How was it?*	Qu'est-ce que tu vas faire samedi prochain? *What are you going to do next Saturday?*	Qu'est-ce que tu vas faire dimanche prochain? *What are you going to do next Sunday?*
e.g.	*Je m'appelle Sébastien.*	*Le week-end dernier, j'ai fait du sport.*	*C'était très épuisant.*	*Samedi prochain, je vais jouer de la batterie.*	*Dimanche prochain, je vais aller faire des courses.*
1.					
2.					
3.					
4.					
5.					
6.					
7.					

UNIT 11 – ANSWERS

FIND SOMEONE WHO

	Find someone who...	Name(s)
1.	...has parents who are going to do sport next Sunday.	**Cédric**
2.	...has a sister who is going to a party next Saturday.	**Jules**
3.	...played the piano last Sunday.	**Cécile**
4.	...played the guitar last Friday.	**Anthony/Hélène**
5.	...played videogames last Sunday.	**François**
6.	...is going to watch a football match next weekend.	**Samuel**
7.	...went to their friend's house last Friday.	**Jean**
8.	...watched a movie at home last weekend.	**Jérôme**
9.	...is going to the shopping mall next weekend.	**Bruno/Stéphane**
10.	...did homework last Sunday.	**Albane/Georges**
11.	...has parents who are going to a party next Sunday.	**Lucas**
12.	...played football last Friday.	**David**
13.	...watched a football match last weekend.	**Myriam**

STAIRCASE TRANSLATION

Le week-end dernier, j'ai vu un match de foot. C'était assez amusant. Samedi prochain, mon frère et moi allons aller à une fête. Dimanche prochain, je vais faire mes devoirs. Ce sera épuisant. Qu'est-ce que tu vas faire le week-end prochain?

FASTER!

REFEREE SOLUTION:

1. Le week-end dernier, j'ai fait du sport.
2. Samedi prochain, je vais aller faire des courses.
3. Ce sera assez intéressant.
4. Dimanche dernier, nous avons vu un match de foot.
5. Vendredi dernier, mon ami et moi avons joué au jeux vidéo.
6. Samedi prochain, ma sœur va aller à un concert.
7. Ce n'était pas amusant du tout.
8. Qu'est-ce que tu vas faire ce week-end?
9. Ce sera très amusant et intéressant.
10. Dimanche prochain, mes parents vont aller à une fête.

FLUENCY CARDS

1. Le week-end prochain, je vais jouer aux jeux vidéo sur mon ordinateur.
2. Dimanche dernier, nous avons joué de la guitare et nous avons vu des films.
3. Vendredi dernier, mon ami(e) et moi avons fait du sport et nous sommes allé(e)s faire des courses.
4. Samedi prochain, je vais faire mes devoirs et je vais voir un match de foot / jouer au foot.
5. Dimanche dernier, ma sœur a joué au basket et elle a joué du piano.
6. Le week-end prochain, je vais aller chez un ami et je vais aller à une fête.

UNIT 12.
Making after-school plans with a friend

Que veux-tu faire *What do you want to do* **Que voulez-vous faire** *What do you guys want to do* **Que voudrais-tu faire** *What would you like to do*	**ce matin?** *this morning?* **cet après-midi?** *this afternoon?* **ce week-end?** *this weekend?*	**aujourd'hui?** *today?* **demain?** *tomorrow?*

Aujourd'hui	**j'aimerais** *I would like to* **je veux** *I want to* **je voudrais** *I would like to*	**aller au cinéma** *go to the cinema* **faire les magasins** *go shopping* **faire un tour en vélo** *go for a bike ride* **jouer au basket** *play basketball*

Voudrais-tu *Would you like to*	**aller au parc** *go to the park* **aller chez Paul** *go to Paul's house* **aller faire un tour en centre-ville** *go for a walk in the centre* **jouer à la PlayStation** *play on the PlayStation*	**avec moi?** *with me?* **avec nous?** *with us?*

Désolé(e), *Sorry,*	**ça ne me dit rien** *I don't fancy it*	**je ne veux pas** *I don't want to*

Oui, *Yes,*	**ça me dit bien, mais** *I fancy it, but* **je voudrais bien, mais** *I would like to, but*	**je ne peux pas** *I can't*	
		je dois *I have to*	**aider ma mère** *help my mother* **étudier** *study* **faire les tâches ménagères** *to do the household chores* **aller chez mes grands-parents** *go to my grandparents' house* **travailler** *work*

Oui, ça me dit bien *Yes, I fancy it*	**Génial!** *Great!*

C'est bon *It's fine* **Pas de problème** *No problem* **D'accord** *OK*	**on peut** *we can*	**aller chez Paul** *go to Paul's house* **aller au stade** *go to the stadium* **jouer à la console** *play on the games console* **rester à la maison** *stay at home*

Fantastique! *Fantastic!* **Génial!** *Great!*	**À quelle heure** *At what time* **Où** *Where*	**on se retrouve?** *shall we meet?*

On se retrouve *Let's meet* **On se voit** *We'll see each other*	**en face** *opposite*	**de chez Paul** **de la poste** **du cinéma**	**à**	**cinq heures** **six heures** **sept heures** / **et quart** **et demie** **moins dix**

Génial, on se voit tout à l'heure *Great, we'll see each other in a while*	**À plus tard** *See you later*

UNIT 12 – FIND SOMEONE WHO – Student Cards

Aujourd'hui, je veux aller au cinéma. **DENIS**	Je veux aller faire un tour en centre-ville. **JADE**	Ce matin, je voudrais faire les magasins. **LÉA**	Aujourd'hui, je voudrais aller au parc. **SERGE**
Je dois faire les tâches ménagères. **CHARLES**	Ce matin, je veux jouer à la console. **JULIEN**	Je veux aller chez mes grands-parents. **VALÉRIE**	Aujourd'hui, je veux aider ma mère. **ANNE**
Cet après-midi, je dois aller chez Paul. **PATRICIA**	Aujourd'hui, j'aimerais aller au parc. **JULIE**	Je voudrais aller au stade. **MICHEL**	Aujourd'hui, je veux jouer au basket. **PAUL**
Aujourd'hui, je veux jouer au basket au parc. **JOËL**	Cet après-midi, je voudrais jouer à la console. **AURORE**	Aujourd'hui, je veux aider ma mère. **CATHERINE**	Cet après-midi, je dois travailler. **PHILIPPE**

UNIT 12 – FIND SOMEONE WHO – Student Grid

Qu'est-ce que tu voudrais faire aujourd'hui?	*What would you like to do today?*	
Find someone who...		**Name(s)**
1.	...wants to play basketball today.	
2.	...would like to go to the stadium today.	
3.	...has to go to Paul's house this afternoon.	
4.	...would like to go to the park today.	
5.	...wants to go to their grandparents' house.	
6.	...wants to go for a walk in the city centre.	
7.	...wants to go to the cinema today.	
8.	...has to work this afternoon.	
9.	...has to do household chores today.	
10.	... would like to go shopping this morning.	
11.	...would like to play on the games console this afternoon.	
12.	...wants to help their mum today.	
13.	...wants to play on their console this morning.	

UNIT 12 – ORAL PING-PONG – Person A

ENGLISH	FRENCH	ENGLISH	FRENCH
What do you want to do this weekend?	Que veux-tu faire ce week-end?	**Yes, I fancy it, but I have to work.**	Oui, ça me dit bien, mais je dois travailler.
Would you like to go to Paul's house with me?		**No problem, we can stay at home.**	
Yes, I would like to, but I have to help my father.	Oui, j'aimerais bien, mais je dois aider mon père.	**Today, I would like to play basketball.**	Aujourd'hui, je voudrais jouer au basket.
Today, I want to go shopping.		**What would you like to do today?**	
What would you like to do this afternoon?	Que voudrais-tu faire cet après-midi?	**Yes, I would like to, but I have to go to my grandparents' house.**	Oui, j'aimerais bien, mais je dois aller chez mes grands-parents.
It's fine, we can go to Paul's house.		**I fancy it, but today I have to study.**	
Today, I would like to go to the cinema.	Aujourd'hui, je voudrais aller au cinéma.	**Yes, I fancy it. Great!**	Oui, ça me dit bien. Génial!
Let's meet opposite the cinema at 6:30.		**Let's meet opposite the shopping mall at 5:00.**	
Today, I would like to go for a bike ride.	Aujourd'hui, je voudrais faire un tour en vélo.	**Yes, I fancy it, but I have to help my mother.**	Oui, ça me dit bien, mais je dois aider ma mère.
Would you like to play on the games console with me?		**Let's meet opposite Pierre's house at 4:50**	

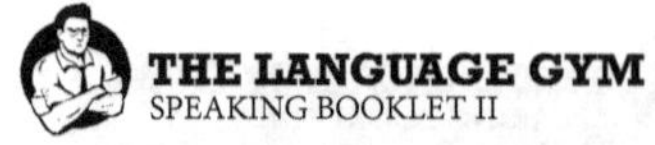

UNIT 12 – ORAL PING-PONG – Person B

ENGLISH	FRENCH	ENGLISH	FRENCH
What do you want to do this weekend?		Yes, I fancy it, but I have to work.	
Would you like to go to Paul's house with me?	Voudrais-tu aller chez Paul avec moi?	No problem, we can stay at home.	Pas de problème, on peut rester à la maison.
Yes, I would like to, but I have to help my father.		Today, I would like to play basketball.	
Today, I want to go shopping.	Aujourd'hui, je veux faire les magasins.	What would you like to do today?	Que voudrais-tu faire aujourd'hui?
What would you like to do this afternoon?		Yes, I would like to, but I have to go to my grandparents' house.	
It's fine, we can go to Paul's house.	C'est bon, on peut aller chez Paul.	I fancy it, but today I have to study.	Ça me dit bien, mais aujourd'hui je dois étudier.
Today, I would like to go to the cinema.		Yes, I fancy it. Great!	
Let's meet opposite the cinema at 6:30.	On se retrouve en face du cinéma à six heures et demie.	Let's meet opposite the shopping mall at 5:00.	On se retrouve en face du centre commercial à cinq heures.
Today, I would like to go for a bike ride.		Yes, I fancy it, but I have to help my mother.	
Would you like to play on the games console with me?	Voudrais-tu jouer à la console avec moi?	Let's meet opposite Pierre's house at 4:50	On se retrouve en face de chez Pierre à cinq heures moins dix.

No Snakes No Ladders

7 What would you like to do today?	**8** Would you like to play on the console with me?	**23** Yes, I fancy it, but I have to help my mum.	**24** Sorry, I don't want to.
6 Today, I would like to go to the cinema.	**9** Yes, I fancy it, but I have to go to my grandparents' house.	**22** Yes, I fancy it. Great!	**25** No problem, we can play on the games console.
5 Yes, I fancy it, but I have to work.	**10** OK, we can play on the console.	**21** Let's meet opposite the shopping mall at 5:00.	**26** Yes, I would like to, but I have to study.
4 Today, I want to go shopping.	**11** Would you like to go to the shopping centre with me?	**20** Yes, I would like to, but I can't.	**27** Let's meet opposite Pierre's house at 5:00.
3 Would you like to go to Paul's house with me?	**12** Fantastic! At what time shall we meet?	**19** Let's meet opposite the cinema at 7:15.	**28** I fancy it today, but I have to study.
2 What would you like to do this afternoon?	**13** No problem, we can stay at home.	**18** Great, we'll see each other in a while.	**29** It's fine, we can go to the stadium.
1 Let's meet opposite the shopping centre at 7:00.	**14** Today, I would like to play basketball.	**17** See you later.	**30** Okay, we can stay at home.
START	**15** It's fine, we can go to Paul's house.	**16** Today, I would like to go shopping.	**FINISH**

No Snakes No Ladders

	1	2	3	4	5	6	7
DÉPART	On se retrouve en face du centre commercial à sept heures.	Que voudrais-tu faire cet après-midi?	Voudrais-tu aller chez Paul avec moi?	Aujourd'hui, je veux faire les magasins.	Oui, ça me dit bien, mais je dois travailler.	Aujourd'hui, je voudrais aller au cinéma.	Que voudrais-tu faire aujourd'hui?
15 C'est bon, on peut aller chez Paul.	**14** Aujourd'hui, je voudrais jouer au basket.	**13** Pas de problème, on peut rester à la maison.	**12** Fantastique! À quelle heure on se retrouve?	**11** Voudrais-tu aller au centre commercial avec moi?	**10** D'accord, on peut jouer à la console.	**9** Oui, ça me dit bien, mais je dois aller chez mes grands-parents.	**8** Voudrais-tu jouer à la console avec moi?
16 Aujourd'hui, je voudrais faire les magasins.	**17** À plus tard.	**18** Génial, on se voit tout à l'heure.	**19** On se retrouve en face du cinéma à sept heures et quart.	**20** Oui, je voudrais bien, mais je ne peux pas.	**21** On se retrouve en face du centre commercial à cinq heures.	**22** Oui, ça me dit bien. Génial!	**23** Oui, ça me dit bien, mais je dois aider ma mère.
ARRIVÉE	**30** D'accord, on peut rester à la maison.	**29** C'est bon, on peut aller au stade.	**28** Ça me dit bien aujourd'hui, mais je dois étudier.	**27** On se retrouve en face de chez Pierre à cinq heures.	**26** Oui, je voudrais bien, mais je dois étudier.	**25** Pas de problème, on peut jouer à la console.	**24** Désolé(e), je ne veux pas.

UNIT 12 – STAIRCASE TRANSLATION

What do you want to do today?

What do you want to do today? Today, I want to go shopping.

What do you want to do today? Today, I want to go shopping. Would you like to go to the mall with me?

What do you want to do today? Today, I want to go shopping. Would you like to go to the mall with me? Yes, I fancy it, but I have to help my mum.

What do you want to do today? Today, I want to go shopping. Would you like to go to the mall with me? Yes, I fancy it, but I have to help my mum. It's fine, we can stay at home.

What do you want to do today? Today, I want go shopping. Would you like to go to the mall with me? Yes, I fancy it, but I have to help my mum. It's fine, we can stay at home. Where shall we meet? Let's meet opposite the cinema at 6:30.

Translate the last step here :

 UNIT 12 – FASTER!

Say:

1. Today, I want to play basketball.

2. Sorry, I don't fancy it.

3. It's fine, we can play on the games console.

4. Yes, I would like to, but I have to work.

5. Great! Where shall we meet?

6. What do you want to do this afternoon?

7. Would you like to go to Paul's house with me?

8. Today, I would like to go for a bike ride.

9. Let's meet opposite the cinema at 5:30.

10. Yes, I fancy it, but I have to do the chores.

	Time	Mistakes	Referee's name
1			
2			
3			
4			

UNIT 12 – FAST & FURIOUS

1. Aujourd'hui, _______ _________________ faire un tour en vélo. (I would like)

2. _______ _________________ aller chez mes grands-parents. (I want)

3. Aujourd'hui, _______ _________________ aller au parc, mais je dois étudier. (I would like)

4. Aujourd'hui, je veux ___________ à la console. (to play)

5. C'est bon, on peut _________ au stade. (to go)

6. Oui, je voudrais bien, mais _____ ___________ ___________ mon père. (I have to help)

7. _____ _____ _________________ en face du cinéma. (Let's meet)

8. Que veux-tu ___________ cet après-midi? (to do)

9. Désolé(e) _____ _____ _________ _______. (I can't)

10. Fantastique! À quelle heure _____ _____ _________________ ? (we meet)

	Time 1	Time 2	Time 3	Time 4
Time				
Mistakes				

UNIT 12 – COMMUNICATIVE DRILLS

1	2	3
What do you want to do this weekend? - I would like to go shopping and to go for a bike ride. **What would you like to do tomorrow?** - Tomorrow, I want to play basketball.	**Would you like to go to the park with me?** - Yes, I fancy it. **Ok, we can go to the park.** - What time shall we meet? **Let's meet opposite my house at 6:00.**	**What do you want to do this afternoon?** - This afternoon, I want to play on the games console. Would you like to play on the console with me? **Yes, I fancy it, but I have to go to my grandparents' house.** - No problem.

4	5	6
Would you like to study tomorrow? - Sorry, I don't fancy it. Would you like to go to the stadium? **Yes, I would like to, but I have to study.** - Ok, we can stay at home and study.	**Today, I want to go to the cinema. Do you want to come with me?** - Yes, I fancy it. Great! At what time shall we meet? **Let's meet opposite the cinema at 5:15.** - Fantastic! See you later.	**Would you like to do the chores?** - Yes, I fancy it, but I have to work. **Ok. Would you like to work with me?** - Ok. Where shall we meet? **Let's meet opposite the shopping mall.**

7	8	9
Do you want to go shopping with me? - Yes, I fancy it. Great! What time shall we meet? **Let's meet opposite the shopping centre at 6:50.** - It's fine. We'll see each other in a while.	**Would you like to go to my grandparents' house with me?** - Yes, I fancy it, but I can't. **Why?** - I have to help my father and I also have to study. **Ok, no problem.**	**What would you like to do tomorrow?** - Tomorrow, I have to go to Paul's house. **Would you like to go for a walk in the city centre with me?** - Yes, I'd like to. **Ok, see you tomorrow.**

UNIT 12 – COMMUNICATIVE DRILLS
REFEREE CARD

1	2	3
Que veux-tu faire ce week-end? - Je voudrais faire les magasins et faire un tour en vélo. **Que voudrais-tu faire demain?** - Demain, je veux jouer au basket.	**Voudrais-tu aller au parc avec moi?** - Oui, ça me dit bien. **D'accord, on peut aller au parc.** - À quelle heure on se retrouve? **On se retrouve en face de chez moi à six heures.**	**Que veux-tu faire cet après-midi?** - Cet après-midi, je veux jouer à la console. Voudrais-tu jouer à la console avec moi? **Oui, ça me dit bien, mais je dois aller chez mes grands-parents.** - Pas de problème.
4	5	6
Voudrais-tu étudier demain? - Désolé(e), ça ne me dit rien. Voudrais-tu aller au stade? **Oui, je voudrais bien, mais je dois étudier.** - D'accord, on peut rester à la maison et étudier.	**Aujourd'hui, je veux aller au cinéma. Veux-tu venir avec moi?** - Oui, ça me dit bien. Génial! À quelle heure on se retrouve? **On se retrouve en face du cinéma à cinq heures et quart.** - Fantastique! À plus tard.	**Voudrais-tu faire les tâches ménagères?** - Oui, ça me dit bien, mais je dois travailler. **D'accord. Voudrais-tu travailler avec moi?** - D'accord. Où on se retrouve? **On se retrouve en face du centre commercial.**
7	8	9
Veux-tu faire les magasins avec moi? - Oui, ça me dit bien. Génial! À quelle heure on se retrouve? **On se retrouve en face du centre commercial à sept heures moins dix.** - C'est bon. On se voit tout à l'heure.	**Voudrais-tu aller chez mes grands-parents avec moi?** - Oui, ça me dit bien, mais je ne peux pas. **Pourquoi?** - Je dois aider mon père et je dois aussi étudier. **D'accord, pas de problème.**	**Qu'est-ce que tu voudrais faire demain?** - Demain, je dois aller chez Paul. **Voudrais-tu faire un tour en centre-ville avec moi?** - Oui, je voudrais bien. **D'accord, à demain.**

UNIT 12 – SURVEY

	Comment tu t'appelles? *What is your name?*	Que veux-tu faire ce week-end? *What do you want to do this weekend?*	Que veux-tu faire demain? *What do you want to do tomorrow?*	Voudrais-tu aller au parc avec moi? *Would you like to go to the park with me?*	Que tu voudrais-tu faire aujourd'hui? *What would you like to do today?*
e.g.	*Je m'appelle Benjamin.*	*Je veux faire les magasins.*	*Demain, je veux jouer au basket.*	*Oui, je voudrais bien, mais aujourd'hui je ne peux pas.*	*Aujourd'hui, je voudrais étudier.*
1.					
2.					
3.					
4.					
5.					
6.					
7.					

UNIT 12 – ANSWERS

FIND SOMEONE WHO

	Find someone who...	Name(s)
1.	...wants to play basketball today.	**Paul/Joël**
2.	...would like to go to the stadium today.	**Michel**
3.	...has to go to Paul's house this afternoon.	**Patricia**
4.	...would like to go to the park today.	**Serge/Julie**
5.	...wants to go to their grandparents' house.	**Valérie**
6.	...wants to go for a walk in the city centre.	**Jade**
7.	...wants to go to the cinema today.	**Denis**
8.	...has to work this afternoon.	**Philippe**
9.	...has to do household chores today.	**Charles**
10.	... would like to go shopping this morning.	**Léa**
11.	...would like to play on the games console this afternoon.	**Aurore**
12.	...wants to help their mum today.	**Anne/Catherine**
13.	...wants to play on their console this morning.	**Julien**

STAIRCASE TRANSLATION

Que veux-tu faire aujourd'hui? Aujourd'hui, je veux faire les magasins. Voudrais-tu aller au centre commercial avec moi? Oui, ça me dit bien, mais je dois aider ma mère. C'est bon, on peut rester à la maison. Où on se retrouve? On se retrouve en face du cinéma à six heures et demie.

FASTER!

REFEREE SOLUTION:

1. Aujourd'hui, je veux jouer au basket.
2. Désolé(e), ça ne me dit rien.
3. C'est bon, on peut jouer à la console.
4. Oui, je voudrais bien, mais je dois travailler.
5. Génial! Où on se retrouve?
6. Que veux-tu faire cet après-midi?
7. Voudrais-tu aller chez Paul avec moi?
8. Aujourd'hui, je voudrais faire un tour en vélo.
9. On se retrouve en face du cinéma à cinq heures et demie.
10. Oui, ça me dit bien, mais je dois faire les tâches ménagères.

FAST & FURIOUS

1. Aujourd'hui, **je voudrais/j'aimerais** faire un tour de vélo.
2. **Je veux** aller chez mes grands-parents.
3. Aujourd'hui, **je voudrais/j'aimerais** aller au parc, mais je dois étudier.
4. Aujourd'hui, je veux **jouer** à la console.
5. C'est bon, on peut **aller** au stade.
6. Oui, je voudrais bien, mais **je dois aider** mon père.
7. **On se retrouve** en face du cinéma.
8. Que veux-tu **faire** cet après-midi?
9. Désolé(e), **je ne peux pas**.
10. Fantastique! À quelle heure **on se retrouve**?

Unit 13. (OPTIONAL)
A future trip to Cannes

Où vas-tu aller cet été?	*Where are you going to go this summer?*
Comment vas-tu voyager?	*How are you going to travel?*
Où vas-tu rester?	*Where are you going to stay?*
Qu'est-ce que tu vas faire?	*What are you going to do?*
Quels endroits vas-tu visiter/voir?	*What places are you going to visit/see?*

Cet été *This summer*	**je vais aller** *I'm going to go*	**à Cannes** *to Cannes*	**Je vais voyager** *I am going to travel* **Nous allons voyager** *We are going to travel*	**en avion** *by plane* **en voiture** *by car*

Le voyage *The trip* **Le vol** *The flight*		**pour la France** *to France*	**dure X heures** *takes X hours*

J'aime *I like* **Je n'aime pas** *I don't like*	**voyager** *to travel*	**en avion** *by plane* **en bateau** *by boat* **en train** *by train* **en voiture** *by car*	**parce que c'est** *because it is*	**amusant** *fun* **bruyant** *noisy* **confortable** *comfortable* **inconfortable** *uncomfortable* **lent** *slow* **rapide** *fast*

À Cannes *In Cannes*	**je vais rester** *I am going to stay* **nous allons rester** *we are going to stay*	**dans** *in*	**un hôtel** *a hotel*	**bon marché** *cheap* **cher** *expensive* **de base** *basic* **de luxe** *luxury*

L'hôtel *The hotel*	**est** *is*	**près** *near* **loin** *far from*	**du Château de Théoule** **du centre-ville** **du Port Canto** **de la plage de la Croisette** **de la vieille ville**	*the Théoule Castle* *the town centre* *the Canto Port* *the Croisette beach* *the old town*

Pendant le voyage...	*During the trip...*

je voudrais *I would like*	**manger** *to eat* **goûter** *to taste/try*	**des fruits de mer** **des plats typiques** **de la bourride (soupe de poisson)**	*seafood* *typical dishes* *local fish soup*
je vais *I'm going*	**faire un tour dans** *to go for a walk around* **visiter** *to visit* **voir** *to see*	**le quartier du Suquet** **la vieille ville** **le Square Mistral** **le jardin botanique** **la Place du Vieux-Port**	*the Suquet neighbourhood* *the old town* *the Mistral Park* *the botanical garden* *the Old Port Square*

Le premier jour *On the first day* **Le deuxième jour** *On the second day* **Le matin** *In the morning* **L'après-midi** *In the afternoon*	**je vais aller** *I am going to go* **nous allons aller** *we are going to go*	**au musée** **au parc** **à la plage** **à un spectacle**	*the museum* *the park* *to the beach* *to a show*

Finalement *Finally*	**je vais** **nous allons**	**rentrer à la maison** *go back home*	**en avion** *by plane* **en car** *by coach*	**en train** *by train* **en voiture** *by car*	

Je crois que le voyage à Cannes sera *I believe the trip to Cannes will be*	**génial** *great* **fantastique** *fantastic*	**inoubliable** *unforgettable* **relaxant** *relaxing*	

J'ai hâte de voyager	*I'm looking forward to travelling*

UNIT 13 – FIND SOMEONE WHO – Student Cards

J'aime voyager en bateau parce que c'est amusant. **YANN**	Je crois que le voyage à Cannes sera génial. **PIERRE**	À Cannes, je vais rester dans un hôtel bon marché. **MÉLANIE**	Je voudrais goûter des plats typiques. **KARINE**
Pendant le voyage, je vais faire un tour dans la vieille ville. **VINCENT**	Le premier jour, je vais aller au parc. **CARMEN**	À Cannes, je vais rester dans un hôtel de base. **LOUISE**	L'après-midi, je vais aller à la plage. **SÉBASTIEN**
Pendant le voyage, je voudrais manger des fruits de mer. **LUCIE**	Je voudrais goûter des plats typiques. **ALAIN**	J'aime voyager en avion parce que c'est confortable. **SARAH**	J'aime voyager en train parce que c'est rapide. **ÉLIANE**
J'aime voyager en avion parce que c'est très rapide. **MATHIEU**	À Cannes, je vais rester dans un hôtel de luxe avec ma famille. **ANTHONY**	Le deuxième jour, nous allons aller au parc. **DAVID**	J'aime voyager en train, même si parfois c'est un peu inconfortable. **MAGALIE**

UNIT 13 – FIND SOMEONE WHO – Student Grid

Comment vas-tu voyager?	*How are you going to travel?*
Où vas-tu rester?	*Where are you going to stay?*

	Find someone who...	Name(s)
1.	...likes to travel by plane.	
2.	...likes to travel by boat.	
3.	...likes to travel by train.	
4.	...is going to stay in a cheap hotel.	
5.	...is going to stay in a basic hotel.	
6.	...is going to stay in a luxury hotel with his family.	
7.	...would like to try typical dishes.	
8.	...would like to eat seafood.	
9.	...is going to go for a walk around the old town.	
10.	...is going to go to the beach in the afternoon.	
11.	...is going to go to the park on the second day.	
12.	...thinks the trip will be great.	
13.	...is going to go to the park on the first day.	

UNIT 13 – ORAL PING-PONG – Person A

ENGLISH	FRENCH	ENGLISH	FRENCH
During the trip, I'm going to visit the Suquet neighbourhood.	Pendant le voyage, je vais visiter le quartier du Suquet.	I'm going to travel by boat.	Je vais voyager en bateau.
Where are you going to go this summer?		The hotel is far from the town centre.	
During the trip, I would like to try seafood.	Pendant le voyage, je voudrais goûter des fruits de mer.	How are you going to travel?	Comment vas-tu voyager?
I like to travel by car because it is comfortable.		I'm going to travel by plane.	
During the trip, I'm going to try typical dishes.	Pendant le voyage, je vais goûter des plats typiques.	In Cannes, I'm going to stay in a basic hotel.	À Cannes, je vais rester dans un hôtel de base.
In the morning, we are going to go to the park.		Finally, we are going to go back home by train.	
In Cannes, I'm going to stay in a luxury hotel.	À Cannes, je vais rester dans un hôtel de luxe.	During the trip, I'm going to try seafood.	Pendant le voyage, je vais goûter des fruits de mer.
What places are you going to visit?		The hotel is far from the old town.	
The hotel is near the Croisette beach.	L'hôtel est près de la plage de la Croisette.	During the trip, I would like to see the botanical garden.	Pendant le voyage, je voudrais voir le jardin botanique.
What are you going to do?		Finally, we are going to go back home by car.	

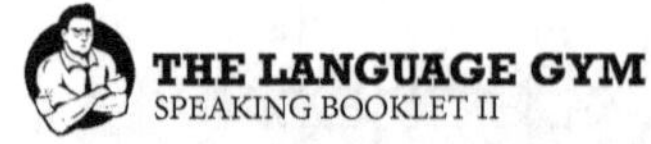

UNIT 13 – ORAL PING-PONG – Person B

ENGLISH	FRENCH	ENGLISH	FRENCH
During the trip, I'm going to visit the Suquet neighbourhood.		I'm going to travel by boat.	
Where are you going to go this summer?	Où vas-tu aller cet été?	The hotel is far from the town centre.	L'hôtel est loin du centre-ville.
During the trip, I would like to try seafood.		How are you going to travel?	
I like to travel by car because it is comfortable.	J'aime voyager en voiture parce que c'est confortable.	I'm going to travel by plane.	Je vais voyager en avion.
During the trip, I'm going to try typical dishes.		In Cannes, I'm going to stay in a basic hostel.	
In the morning, we are going to go to the park.	Le matin, nous allons aller au parc.	Finally, we are going to go back home by train.	Finalement, nous allons rentrer à la maison en train.
In Cannes, I'm going to stay in a luxury hotel.		During the trip, I'm going to try seafood.	
What places are you going to visit?	Quels endroits vas-tu visiter?	The hotel is far from the old town.	L'hôtel est loin de la vieille ville.
The hotel is near the Croisette beach.		During the trip, I would like to see the botanical garden.	
What are you going to do?	Qu'est-ce que tu vas faire?	Finally, we are going to go back home by car.	Finalement, nous allons rentrer à la maison en voiture.

No Snakes No Ladders

START

1. What places are you going to visit?
2. During the trip, I'm going to try seafood.
3. Where are you going to stay?
4. During the trip, I'm going to try typical dishes.
5. During the trip, I would like to see the botanical garden.
6. In the afternoon, I'm going to go to a show.
7. I am going to travel by plane.
8. In Cannes, I'm going to stay in a basic hotel.
9. Finally, we are going to go back home by train.
10. I am going to travel by car.
11. The hotel is far from the old town.
12. During the trip, I would like to visit the park.
13. Finally, we are going to go back home by car.
14. During the trip, I'm going to eat typical dishes.
15. The hotel is near the town centre.
16. I don't like to travel by boat because it's slow and expensive.
17. During the trip, I would like to go for a walk around the old town.
18. The hotel is far from the town centre.
19. During the trip, I would like to try seafood.
20. Where are you going to go this summer?
21. We are not going to stay in an expensive hotel.
22. What are you going to do?
23. The hotel is near the Croisette beach.
24. I am not going to stay in a basic hotel.
25. On the second day, I am going to go to the museum with my dad.
26. The hotel is far from the beach.
27. How are you going to travel?
28. I like to travel by train because it's fast.
29. I like to travel by plane because it's comfortable.
30. On the second day, we are going to go to the beach.

FINISH

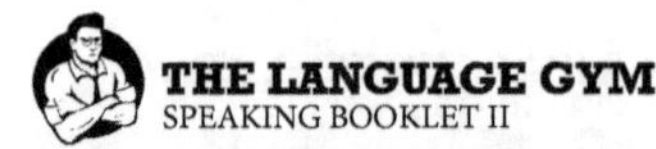
THE LANGUAGE GYM
SPEAKING BOOKLET II

No Snakes No Ladders

7 Je vais voyager en avion.	**6** L'après-midi, je vais aller à un spectacle.	**5** Pendant le voyage, je voudrais voir le jardin botanique.	**4** Pendant le voyage, je vais goûter des plats typiques.	**3** Où vas-tu rester?
8 À Cannes, je vais rester dans un hôtel de base.	**9** Finalement, nous allons rentrer à la maison en train.	**10** Je vais voyager en voiture.	**11** L'hôtel est loin de la vieille ville.	**12** Pendant le voyage, je voudrais visiter le parc.
23 L'hôtel est près de la plage de la Croisette.	**22** Qu'est-ce que tu vas faire?	**21** Nous n'allons pas rester dans un hôtel cher.	**20** Où vas-tu aller cet été?	**19** Pendant le voyage, je voudrais goûter des fruits de mer.
24 Je ne vais pas rester dans un hôtel de base.	**25** Le deuxième jour, je vais aller au musée avec mon père.	**26** L'hôtel est loin de la plage.	**27** Comment vas-tu voyager?	**28** J'aime voyager en train parce que c'est rapide.

2 Pendant le voyage, je vais goûter des fruits de mer.	**1** Quels endroits vas-tu visiter?
13 Finalement, nous allons rentrer à la maison en voiture.	**14** Pendant le voyage, je vais manger des plats typiques.
18 L'hôtel est loin du centre-ville.	**17** Pendant le voyage, je voudrais faire un tour dans la vieille ville.
29 J'aime voyager en avion parce que c'est confortable.	**30** Le deuxième jour, nous allons aller à la plage.

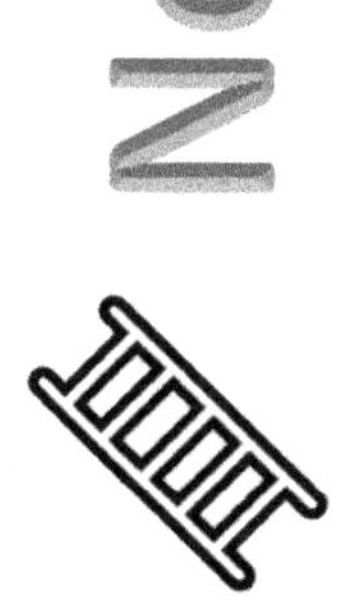

DÉPART

15 L'hôtel est près du centre-ville.

16 Je n'aime pas voyager en bateau parce que c'est lent et cher.

ARRIVÉE

UNIT 13 – STAIRCASE TRANSLATION

This summer, I'm going to go to Cannes. We're going to travel by plane.

This summer, I'm going to go to Cannes. We're going to travel by plane because it is comfortable. The flight to France takes three hours.

This summer, I'm going to go to Cannes. We're going to travel by plane because it is comfortable. The flight to France takes three hours. In Cannes I'm going to stay in an expensive hotel.

This summer, I'm going to go to Cannes. We're going to travel by plane because it is comfortable. The flight to France takes three hours. In Cannes, I'm going to stay in an expensive hotel. The hotel is near to the old town.

This summer, I'm going to go to Cannes. We're going to travel by plane because it is comfortable. The flight to France takes three hours. In Cannes, I'm going to stay in an expensive hotel. The hotel is near to the old town. During the trip, I would like to try typical dishes.

This summer, I'm going to go to Cannes. We're going to travel by plane because it is comfortable. The flight to France takes three hours. In Cannes, I'm going to stay in an expensive hotel. The hotel is near to the old town. During the trip, I would like to try typical dishes. I believe the trip to Cannes will be unforgettable.

Translate the last step here:

⏱ UNIT 13 – FASTER! 🐦

Say:

1. This summer, I'm going to go to Cannes.

2. I am going to travel by car.

3. I like to travel by boat because it is fun.

4. We are going to stay in a cheap hotel.

5. The hotel is near the Canto Port.

6. During the trip, I would like to eat seafood.

7. I'm going to go for a walk around the botanical garden.

8. On the first day, I'm going to go to the beach.

9. Finally, we are going to go back home by coach.

10. I'm looking forward to travelling.

	Time	Mistakes	Referee's name
1			
2			
3			
4			

UNIT 13 – THINGS IN COMMON

Write your own answers to the questions then interview four friends and make a note of what things you have in common.

Qu'est-ce que tu préfères?	Moi (Your own answer)	1	2	3	4
Voyager en voiture ou en avion?					
Aller en vacances en France ou en Espagne?					
Rester dans un hôtel de luxe ou dans un hôtel bon marché?					
Manger des fruits de mer ou de la soupe de poisson?					
Visiter la vieille ville ou le jardin botanique?					
Aller à la plage ou au parc?					
Aller voir un spectacle ou un match de foot?					

UNIT 13 – COMMUNICATIVE DRILLS

1	2	3
Where are you going to go this summer? - This summer, I'm going to go to France. **How are you going to travel?** - I like to travel by plane because it's fast and comfortable. However, we're going to travel by train.	**Where are you going to go this summer?** - This summer, I'm going to go to France with my family. **Great! Where are you going to stay?** - We're going to stay in a luxury hotel. It's close to the beach.	**What places are you going to visit?** - I'm going to visit the old town and the Suquet neighbourhood. **Are you going to go for a walk around the old town?** - Yes, I would like to. It will be unforgettable.
4	**5**	**6**
What do you want to do in France? - I want to go to a show in the town centre. **Where are you going to stay?** - I'm going to stay in a hotel near the town square. **Great! It will be fantastic.**	**This summer, I'm going to go to Portugal with my friends. And you?** - I'm going to Portugal, too. I'm going to try typical dishes. On the first day, I'm going to go to the beach. On the second day, I'm going to visit the museum.	**How are you going to travel to France?** - We're going to travel by boat. The trip to France takes twelve hours. It's slow! **What are you going to do during your trip?** - On the first day, we're going to go to the town centre. On the second day, we're going to visit the botanical garden.
7	**8**	**9**
What are you going to do in Cannes? - On the first day, in the morning, I'm going to go the park. In the afternoon, we're going to go the museum. Finally, we're going to go back home by coach. **I think the trip will be unforgettable.**	**What places are you going to visit?** - I'm going to visit the old town and the port. **What are you going to do?** - I'm going to eat seafood and I am going to try typical dishes. I'd like to try fish soup.	**I'm going to take a walk around the old town and see the botanical garden. And you?** - We're going to stay in an expensive hotel near the town centre. I'd like to visit the museum.

UNIT 13 – COMMUNICATIVE DRILLS
REFEREE CARD

<table>
<tr><td colspan="1">

1

Où vas-tu aller cet été?

- Cet été, je vais aller en France.

Comment vas-tu voyager?

- J'aime voyager en avion parce que c'est rapide et confortable. Cependant, nous allons voyager en train.

</td><td colspan="1">

2

Où vas-tu aller cet été?

- Cet été, je vais aller en France avec ma famille.

Génial! Où vas-tu rester?

- Nous allons rester dans un hôtel de luxe. C'est près de la plage.

</td><td colspan="1">

3

Quels endroits vas-tu visiter?

- Je vais visiter la vieille ville et le quartier du Suquet.

Tu vas faire un tour dans la vieille ville?

- Oui, je voudrais bien. Ce sera inoubliable.

</td></tr>
<tr><td>

4

Que veux-tu faire en France?

- Je veux aller à un spectacle en centre-ville.

Où vas-tu rester?

- Je vais rester dans un hôtel près de la place.

Génial! Ce sera fantastique.

</td><td>

5

Cet été, je vais aller au Portugal avec mes amis. Et toi?

- Je vais aussi aller au Portugal. Je vais goûter des plats typiques. Le premier jour, je vais aller à la plage. Le deuxième jour, je vais visiter le musée.

</td><td>

6

Comment vas-tu voyager en France?

- Nous allons voyager en bateau. Le voyage pour la France dure douze heures. C'est lent!

Qu'est-ce que tu vas faire pendant ton voyage?

- Le premier jour, nous allons aller au centre-ville. Le deuxième jour, nous allons visiter le jardin botanique.

</td></tr>
<tr><td>

7

Qu'est-ce que tu vas faire à Cannes?

- Le premier jour, le matin, je vais aller au parc. L'après-midi, nous allons aller au musée. Finalement, nous allons rentrer à la maison en car.

Je pense que le voyage sera inoubliable.

</td><td>

8

Quels endroits vas-tu visiter?

- Je vais visiter la vieille ville et le port.

Qu'est-ce que tu vas faire?

- Je vais manger des fruits de mer et je vais goûter des plats typiques. Je voudrais goûter de la soupe de poisson.

</td><td>

9

Je vais faire un tour dans la vieille ville et voir le jardin botanique. Et toi?

- Nous allons rester dans un hôtel cher près du centre-ville. Je voudrais visiter le musée.

</td></tr>
</table>

UNIT 13 – SURVEY

	Comment tu t'appelles? *What is your name?*	**Où vas-tu aller cet été?** *Where are you going to go this summer?*	**Comment vas-tu voyager?** *How are you going to travel?*	**Où vas-tu rester?** *Where are you going to stay?*	**Qu'est-ce que tu vas faire?** *What are you going to do?*	**Quels endroits vas-tu visiter?** *What places are you going to visit?*
e.g.	*Je m'appelle Michel.*	*Cet été, je vais aller en France.*	*Je vais voyager en voiture.*	*Je vais rester dans un hôtel de luxe.*	*Le premier jour, je vais aller à la plage.*	*Je vais visiter la vieille ville.*
1.						
2.						
3.						
4.						
5.						
6.						
7.						

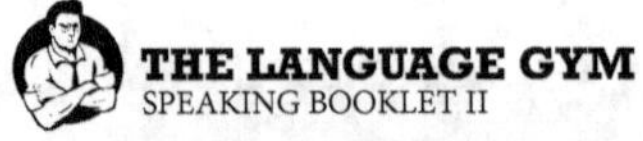

UNIT 13 – ANSWERS

FIND SOMEONE WHO

	Find someone who...	Name(s)
1.	...likes to travel by plane.	**Sarah/Mathieu**
2.	...likes to travel by boat.	**Yann**
3.	...likes to travel by train.	**Éliane/Magalie**
4.	...is going to stay in a cheap hotel.	**Mélanie**
5.	...is going to stay in a basic hotel.	**Louise**
6.	...is going to stay in a luxury hotel with his family.	**Anthony**
7.	...would like to try typical dishes.	**Karine/Alain**
8.	...would like to eat seafood.	**Lucie**
9.	...is going to go for a walk around the old town.	**Vincent**
10.	...is going to go to the beach in the afternoon.	**Sébastien**
11.	...is going to go to the park on the second day.	**David**
12.	...thinks the trip will be great.	**Pierre**
13.	...is going to go to the park on the first day.	**Carmen**

STAIRCASE TRANSLATION

Cet été, je vais aller à cannes. Nous allons voyager en avion parce que c'est confortable. Le vol pour la France dure trois heures. À Cannes, je vais rester dans un hôtel cher. L'hôtel est près de la vieille ville. Pendant le voyage, je voudrais goûter des plats typiques. Je crois que le voyage à Cannes sera inoubliable.

FASTER!

REFEREE SOLUTION:
1. Cet été, je vais aller à Cannes.
2. Je vais voyager en voiture.
3. J'aime voyager en bateau parce que c'est amusant.
4. Nous allons rester dans un hôtel bon marché.
5. L'hôtel est près du Port Canto.
6. Pendant le voyage, je voudrais manger des fruits de mer.
7. Je vais faire un tour dans le jardin botanique.
8. Le premier jour, je vais aller à la plage.
9. Finalement, nous allons rentrer à la maison en car.
10. J'ai hâte de voyager.

THINGS IN COMMON

Students give their own answers to the questions and make a note of which students they have things in common with.